WILLIAM HENRY JACKSON:

Pioneer Photographer of the West

Also by Aylesa Forsee

LOUIS AGASSIZ: *Pied Piper of Science*

WILLIAM HENRY
JACKSON ~ *Pioneer*

Photographer of the West

by AYLESA FORSEE   *Illustrated with*
Drawings by DOUGLAS GORSLINE, *and with*
Photographs by WILLIAM HENRY JACKSON

New York
THE VIKING PRESS

*Dedicated to Clarence Seymour Jackson,
who shared letters, diaries, photographs,
scrapbooks, and a son's memories
to make his father come alive for me*

Acknowledgments

The author acknowledges her indebtedness to the Western History Library at the University of Colorado and to the Western Division of the Denver Public Library for their interest and assistance in the preparation of this book.

Grateful acknowledgment is made to the following for courtesy in permitting the use of photographs by William Henry Jackson:

George Eastman House, Rochester, New York: William Henry Jackson and his assistant at the Grand Tetons, 1872; Crater of Old Faithful, Yellowstone National Park.

Explorers Club of New York: The Grand Teton.

Clarence S. Jackson and Basil Zeigler for photographs from the William Henry Jackson File: Hayden Survey en route, 1871; Mount of the Holy Cross; Cliff Palace, Mesa Verde (before restoration); William Henry Jackson and friend.

Bureau of American Ethnology, Smithsonian Institution: Pottery maker, pueblo of Tewa; Brothers, from Kitkehahki or Republican Pawnee band;

Library, State Historical Society of Colorado: California big trees, "Haverford"; San Francisco waterfront, 1900.

Western History Department, Denver Public Library: On Hayden Survey; Quarry at Wilson's Spur; Railroad operations near Buena Vista, Colorado; Green River Butte, Wyoming; Denver–Rio Grande train in Las Animas Canyon.

U.S. Geological Survey: First photograph ever made of Old Faithful, Yellowstone National Park; Packing a wagon across the San Juan Mountains; Campsight in the foothills of the Uinta

Mountains, 1870; Camp at Three Springs, Bannock County, Idaho; Mammoth Hot Springs, Yellowstone National Park; Jackson Canyon, now known as Sheep Canyon, Natrona County, Wyoming; Natural Bridge, La Prele Canyon, Converse County, Wyoming.

Contents

10   Contents

List of Illustrations

Foreword

WILLIAM HENRY JACKSON bullwhacked across the plains, herded wild horses from Los Angeles to Omaha, journeyed across Korea when bandits infested that land, and sledged across Siberia. Wherever he went, whatever he did, he kept a record with sketches or photographs. During his lifetime he used every kind of camera, from the ones required for the daguerreotypy process in use during the 1840s, to the modern light-weight Leica.

Jackson's photographs of the Yellowstone area, taken at a time when trappers and Indians still regarded it as an infernal region, helped win Congressional approval for establishment of the first national park. He gave stereoscope owners their first views of the long-lost cities of cliff dwellers in the Mesa Verde region of Colorado. His photographs of the Holy Cross Mount proved the existence of a phenomenon which previously had been considered legendary. Pictures he took under the auspices of many railroads made Americans aware of the spaciousness, grandeur, and beauty of their land.

These, as well as portraits of Hopis, coolies, maharajahs, Mongolian fishermen, and Siberian prisoners, brought Jackson

13

many awards and world-wide fame. Paintings that he completed during the 1930s, when he served as research secretary for the Oregon Trail Memorial Association, recreated dramatic incidents of bullwhacking, pony express, and pioneer days.

Besides being a photographer and painter, Jackson was an author, explorer, and popular after-dinner speaker. But it is as a recorder of the vanished West that he occupies a unique position. His photographs are carefully preserved in museums. His paintings hang in railroad terminals, libraries, schools, universities, urban and national park museums. The country he loved will not soon forget the contributions of William Henry Jackson—cameraman, recorder, explorer—an artist in his paintings and his life.

TWENTY-THREE PHOTOGRAPHS

by William Henry Jackson

Hayden Survey en route, 1871

Mount of the Holy Cross, 1873

[18]

Cliff Palace, Mesa Verde (before restoration)

First photograph ever made of Old Faithful, Yellowstone National Park

Packing a wagon across the San Juan Mountains

Pottery maker, pueblo of Tewa

On Hayden Survey

Campsite in the foothills of the Uinta Mountains, 1870

Quarry at Wilson's Spur

California big trees, "Haverford"

San Francisco waterfront, 1900

Railroad operations near Buena Vista, Colorado

Green River Butte, Wyoming

Denver – Rio Grande train in Las Animas Canyon

The Grand Teton

Brothers, from Kitkehahki or Republican Pawnee band

[37]

Camp at Three Springs, Bannock County, Idaho

Mammoth Hot Springs, Yellowstone National Park

Jackson Canyon, now known as Sheep Canyon, Natrona County, Wyoming

Natural Bridge, La Prele Canyon, Converse County, Wyoming

William Henry Jackson and his assistant at the Grand Tetons, 1872

Crater of Old Faithful, Yellowstone National Park

Clarence Jackson always called this picture
"William Henry Jackson and friend"

WILLIAM HENRY JACKSON:

Pioneer Photographer of the West

Gorsline

W. H. Jackson at 17—
photographer's apprentice

1: *Sign Painter to Soldier*

ALONE in the bare room over the family woodshed, William Henry Jackson added the last letter to a sign reading:

> Death to all vermin.
> Use Costar's rat, roach,
> and bug exterminator.

As he finished the card ordered by a local drugstore, Bill stood up and unkinked his muscles. His restless, clear blue

49

eyes darted to a dusty camera standing on a tripod in one corner of the room. Maybe he could earn more money by taking pictures, he thought, tugging at a defiant lock of brown hair. If only he knew the mechanism of the new wet-plate photographic process. His father, a blacksmith and carriage maker, had taught him a little about daguerreotypy, but the citizens of Troy, New York, no longer wanted silver-plated photographs.

Bill's attention was drawn away from finances and photography when nine-year-old Mary Elizabeth called from the bottom of the stairway. "It's suppertime and Mama says to hurry."

Bill clattered down the steps and into the big yard between the shed and the house.

"Race you!" called his brother Ed.

Breathing in great lungfuls of moist April air, Bill streaked ahead of his younger brother into the kitchen, where Mrs. Jackson forked fried chicken onto a platter. Mr. Jackson supervised Fred and Frank, aged seven and five, as they washed up for supper.

At the supper table Mr. Jackson spoke regretfully of disputes over slavery that had arisen between the northern and southern states. Because the family had lived in both sections of the country, Bill hardly knew on which side his sympathy lay. Born in Keeseville, New York, on April 4, 1843, he had been taken by his parents to Columbus, Georgia, then to Plattsburgh, New York. From there the family had moved to a farm, then to Petersburg, Virginia, to Philadelphia, and finally to Troy.

Next day as Bill went to deliver his posters he was thinking that he was almost old enough to enlist, if the quarrel between the North and the South did get to the fighting stage.

But he forgot the rumors of war when the druggist, Mr. Johnson, after critically examining the bug-exterminator display card, suggested, "Why don't you see Schoonmaker? He needs an assistant to do some water-coloring."

C. C. Schoonmaker was Troy's leading photographer. Bill hardly dared hope the photographer would hire an amateur painter, but he set off for the studio. On the way he remembered how his mother had supervised his early attempts at drawing, when his horses had stilt legs and his rivers ran uphill. Did he have the talent that this job required?

"What I need," Schoonmaker told Bill, "is a retoucher. Water colors lend warmth to black-and-white prints, but"— the photographer frowned as he studied Bill's face—"aren't you a little young?"

"I'll be fifteen day after tomorrow," Bill told him, trying to appear mature and competent.

Schoonmaker smiled. "Want to start tomorrow?" he asked.

Everything about the studio fascinated Bill. While he washed color over black-and-white prints, he learned all he could about photographic procedures. Some day, Bill promised himself, he would have a business of his own.

School seemed dull compared to the studio. Bill had heard all he cared to know about how Henry Hudson in his ship the *Half Moon* had come up the river named for him as far as Troy.

During the summer of 1858 Bill played one-o'-cat less often

than usual. Having a career made him feel years older than his former schoolmates. Occasionally he shed his new-found maturity and prowled with his buddies along the waterfront, looking at tugboats and barges. He went on picnics; he made sketches. That fall when several of his friends went on to college he wondered if his decision to work had been the right one. But the country needed men, not schoolboys, he told himself, when he read the sobering details of the North-South squabble.

Another year passed, and by the fall of 1860, hostility had heightened. Although he was not old enough to vote, Bill campaigned for his presidential choice, Abraham Lincoln. On the eve of the election in November, he joined a parade in which almost every marcher carried a torch. Led by a band playing spirited tunes, Bill and his friends made their way to the hilly campus of Rensselaer Polytechnic Institute, where they set off Roman candles that fizzed fire and color.

The following month, Frank Mowrey, a photographer from Rutland, Vermont, visited Schoonmaker's. He interviewed Bill and offered him a position at six dollars a week. Elated at the prospect, Bill charged out of the studio and rushed home to tell his family.

"You'll spend most of what you make on living expenses," his father warned.

"And Vermont is awfully far away," Mary Elizabeth said in a shaky voice.

Bill, who had calmed down somewhat, patted his sister on the shoulder. "I'll come home on visits," he promised.

Not until the train neared the marble quarries outside Rutland did Bill begin to have misgivings. How was he going to manage things his mother had always done for him, things like laundry? Would he make new friends easily?

Bill liked working for the mild, agreeable Mr. Mowrey, who willingly answered questions about cameras and demonstrated photographic processes. For customers who wanted backgrounds more unusual than columns or tasseled draperies, Bill painted scenes such as Niagara Falls or ancient Athens.

The hours in the studio passed quickly, though at first he was homesick when he went home to his rented room. He took art lessons and read J. G. Chapman's *American Drawing Book*. From Chapman he learned the mysteries of perspective, the rules of composition and design, the laws of color values, and how to model. He made friends in Rutland, and when summer came there were parties and fishing trips or picnics on the pine-clad slopes of the Green Mountains.

New Year's Day of 1861 ushered in a period of national tumult. South Carolina had already seceded from the Union, and other states were soon to follow. In April the Confederates seized Fort Sumter, which dominated Charleston Harbor. Close on the heels of this stunning news came the announcement by President Lincoln that the North would defend its principles. This meant war, thought Bill, half dismayed, half relieved that the conflict had finally come to a head.

At first the clash of arms seemed remote. Then in July came news of the battle of Bull Run. A Rebel army had sent raw, untrained Federal recruits into disorderly retreat. Bill, by now sure of his loyalty to the Union and to Lincoln, wrote home to get permission to enlist.

His mother, a Friend, opposed his plan. War, she said, was contrary to Quaker beliefs. Mr. Jackson advised him to stick to his job for the time being.

That fall a phrenologist, Orson Squire Fowler, came to Rutland. Bill and his friends went for "readings." After feeling the bumps on Bill's skull, the phrenologist told him that he had a noble head, a love of beauty, and splendid talents. "But you should take care of your bodily powers," he cautioned. Mr. Fowler concluded the reading by saying, "You are really a genius and no mistake."

Impressed by the warning that he should get more exercise, Bill bought a pair of heavy Indian clubs, which he swung vigorously every day all winter long. Meanwhile, the Union met with more reverses than victories. Lincoln called for volunteers. When Bill once more urged his parents to consent to his enlistment, they wrote back, "Use your own judgment."

His country, Bill realized, was worth defending, even if it meant exchanging his drawing pencil and his dreams for a musket and army routines. He applied for membership in the Rutland Light Guard, a part of the state militia, which planned to offer its services to the nation.

2: *Bivouacs, Bullets, and Billets*

IN SEPTEMBER 1862, Bill and his brother Ed, who had come to enlist in the Vermont Volunteers, began their military training in Rutland. Three weeks later, the brothers were transferred to an army camp at Brattleboro. When reveille sounded at six o'clock each morning, Bill dressed quickly. Then, shivering and still half asleep, he walked out into the uninviting half light to a day of marching and musket toting.

A reward for the hours of drilling and obeying orders came a little over a month later when Bill and Ed assembled with their buddies to be mustered into the United States Army as members of Company K of the Twelfth Regiment. The following week the Vermont Volunteers, as the Twelfth Regiment was known, fell into parade formation to march to the Brattleboro railroad station. They were bound for Dixie. Flags fluttered above buildings draped in red, white, and blue bunting. Onlookers cheered.

Bill felt like a conquering hero. But he felt less heroic when the soldiers arrived at the station and found no transportation awaiting them. Finally a freight train came, and the men, joking among themselves, crowded into the boxcars and rattled off into the night.

Not until four days later did the Vermonters reach Washington, D.C. When they had a few hours of leave, Bill, Ed, and their friend Ned Birdsall went sightseeing. Bill was disappointed in the nation's capital when he saw geese detouring around piles of garbage. Hogs wallowed in a street that had become a sea of liquid mud after a rain.

But later, when he went to a session of Congress, met members of the Cabinet on the street, and heard the shrill-voiced newsboys shouting the latest presidential decision, it seemed to Bill that he could almost hear the heartbeat of the nation.

Orders to leave Washington came on October 29. The Vermonters struck their tents, shouldered equipment, and trudged off down Pennsylvania Avenue. Broken cobblestones hurt Bill's feet. Besides his extra clothes and art supplies, all rolled into his blankets, he carried a musket, a leather cartridge box with ammunition, and a pouch of percussion caps to ignite powder. On his left hip rode a bayonet, which so far had been used only as a digging tool or a spit for cooking meat over a campfire. His canteen and cup clanked alongside his haversack.

As they marched out across Long Bridge, a brick causeway into Virginia, Bill and his companions sang, "We are coming, Father Abraham, three hundred thousand more." The song went on to lines about leaving plows, workshops, wives, and children.

Some twelve miles beyond Washington, Company K pitched camp. Bill knew he now stood on the soil of the Confederacy.

At any moment a cannon might lob death-dealing shells into their ranks.

"Your assignment," the commanding officer intoned, "will be to picket the woods beyond the Potomac River and prevent a surprise attack on Washington."

Each day Bill worked with pick and shovel on a fort, stood sentry duty, and drilled. Winter came early that year, and the shivering Vermonters went around in wet clothes much of the time. Finally, the commanding officer doled out axes to use in building shelters.

Bill, Ed, and their friends Ned Birdsall and Charley Huntoon put up mud-caked log walls three feet high and then used their tent as a roof. Boxes served as seats. From a deserted farmhouse the soldiers salvaged bricks and built a little stove, for which the woods around them provided plenty of fuel.

At night in the feeble glow cast by a candle set in a bayonet socket, they played cards or talked about their families, sweethearts, and the great country opening up beyond the Mississippi River. But almost always their conversation turned to the war and the names of places that had once meant homes and farms but now meant battlegrounds.

To eke out army rations, the tentmates went foraging. Once they found frost-nipped persimmons. The plumlike fruit had a tangy taste and was a welcome addition to salt pork, bean soup, and the thin biscuit known as hardtack—always hard, and often stale or wormy.

Company K's assignment to picket duty meant immunity from battlefield casualties, but several young men died of exposure or disease. During the move to a new campsite, Bill saw the aftereffects of war—buildings burned or halfway torn down, woods blighted and scarred.

One December morning the order, "Be ready to march at a moment's notice," electrified the camp.

"The Rebs must really be pushing us," Ed said uneasily when Company K marched off—not toward the South, but toward Washington.

A short time later, orders came to halt and make a stand. Some soldiers manned the breastworks. Others took charge of the cannons trained on the road.

"Expect an attack any minute now," General Stoughton warned as he rode up and down the lines on a handsome mount.

Almost at once shots were heard. Not more than a hundred yards away Bill could see the flash of the guns of Confederate soldiers. With musket aimed he lay in breathless silence waiting for the charge that would surely come. But there was no further action.

That night Bill and the others, chilled to the bone, huddled together trying to get warm. Around midnight they heard General Stoughton shout, "Battle stations!" Bill, his muscles cramped, his teeth chattering from cold and suspense, moved stiffly to his post. Sleep made his eyes heavy, but he forced himself into wary watchfulness. Nothing, he thought, made the hours seem so long as did fear. Again no muskets fired, and at dawn General Stoughton ordered Company K back to camp.

The early days of 1863 brought other false alarms. To camp

came reports that the South was inflicting bloody losses and that the federal treasury was almost empty. Trying to forget all this dreariness, Bill spent much of his spare time drawing. In each letter he mailed to his family or friends he included a scene of camp life. He mailed cards with drawings and pictures so often that he has been called the innovator of picture post-cards. He also penciled portraits of young men growing beards for the first time, who wanted to send home proof of their manliness.

One afternoon Bill received a summons to see Colonel Blunt. He liked the Colonel but knew he could be severe. The summons must mean he was in for a reprimand.

Almost as soon as Bill stepped inside the tent, Colonel Blunt said, "Jackson, from now on I want you to draw."

"Draw?" echoed Bill, startled but relieved. "What do you want me to draw, sir?"

"A record of camp life." Blunt drummed his fingers on the table at which he was sitting. "As a staff artist," he said, "you will be relieved of ordinary fatigue duty and be entitled to eat at the orderlies' mess."

When Bill left the tent he swaggered a bit. The title of staff artist sounded impressive.

Six days later Colonel Blunt sent for him again. Bill exhibited his drawings of the camp and the lay of the land surrounding it.

Colonel Blunt let out a low whistle. "Splendid!" he said appreciatively. "A dependable ground plan is most helpful in planning breastworks and strategy."

Early in April, just before his twentieth birthday, Bill was

working on a map of Bull Run Creek. Following the left
bank, he came to a spot so marshy he could not continue on
foot. He was about to turn back when he saw a crude log
raft at the edge of the stream. Just what I need, he said to
himself.

Then he hesitated a moment. Across Bull Run lay enemy
territory and the raft would make an excellent target, but he
decided he'd risk it. Bill poled out into deep water. Then,
sitting cross-legged, he let the raft drift slowly down the
sluggish stream while he sketched. For a mile or so he noted
curves, marked clumps of willows or oaks. Rounding a
wooded bend he heard the cock of a musket. His pulse
pounded unevenly.

"Who goes there?" a voice asked sharply.

"F—friend," stammered Bill. But he feared that the picket
who had challenged him was far from friendly. The raft
must have drifted into Reb-controlled land.

As he maneuvered his clumsy raft toward the shore, Bill
saw that the sentries who had challenged him wore uniforms
like his own. But they insisted on taking him to their squad
sergeant.

"Satisfactory," the sergeant said, after examining Bill's pass.
"But your behavior in riding down a stream in full view of
the enemy was careless, to say the least."

"Yes, sir," Bill replied meekly. In the future he'd be a more
alert soldier, he promised as he returned to camp.

There seemed to be little need for alertness during the
sultry summer weeks that followed. However, on June 30 an
insistent bugle roused Company K at four-thirty in the morning

to set off on a twenty-mile march. The men were dirt-encrusted and footsore at the end of the day. "I hope we don't have to fight any Rebs tonight," Bill said wearily as he bit into his hardtack.

"The rumor is that Lee has made a thrust into Pennsylvania," said his friend Ruel Rounds. "My guess is that we'll meet the Rebs head on."

Next morning, slogging along through a chilling rain, Bill had the feeling that something ominous hovered nearby. Today or tomorrow he might be fighting for his life, might even lose it.

Jackson at 22—
Vermont photographer

3: *Shattered Plans*

ABOUT four miles from Gettysburg, Pennsylvania, Bill's commanding officer called a halt and announced that Company K would stay behind the battle lines to guard the baggage. When the company started forward again the men on foot almost had to run to keep up with the supplies being hauled in wagons at the greatest possible speed. At intervals Rebel sharpshooters fired at the wagon train and then disappeared. Not until eleven o'clock that night did Company K reach its temporary camp.

Next morning heavy cannonading came from the direction of Gettysburg. Did fellow Vermonters on the shot-torn hillside at Cemetery Ridge feel heroic or terrified? Bill wondered.

Where did fear leave off and courage begin? Hoping to take his mind off the turmoil within himself, he unwrapped his pencils and paper and began to draw, but he couldn't keep his mind on his work.

News came on July 4 that Lee's forces had been outnumbered and outmaneuvered. But at Vicksburg the Union had suffered heavy casualties. Many of the Vermonters who had marched forth to the battle would never return.

To Company K fell the task of escorting 2300 Rebel prisoners to Fort McHenry. Bill found it hard to believe that these haggard, exhausted men were supposed to be his enemies.

After the prisoners of war had been consigned, the whole Twelfth Regiment, their term of service completed, started north to Vermont. As he rode northward with his company perched on the top of a swaying boxcar, Bill came to the conclusion that he had gained more from military service than he had given. Camp life had toughened his body and taught him to do without luxuries. He had learned to get along with all kinds of people and had made what he hoped would be friends for a lifetime.

When Bill and Ed arrived home in Troy, several days after receiving their honorable discharges, the family greeted them with admiration and bear hugs. At first Bill wanted to do little except eat, sleep, and get acquainted with his youngest brother Allen, who had been born during the war. When he woke up in the mornings he lay in bed gloating that there'd be no summons from a bugle, no sentry duty, no forced marches. By the end of a week, however, he and Ed had

had enough of loafing. Ed decided to re-enlist, but Bill returned to Mr. Mowrey's studio in Rutland.

For a time he missed the suspense of wartime camps. Most of all he missed the closeness of comrades facing a common crisis. But he liked his work and added to his studio salary by taking orders for oil paintings, mostly portraits, and by giving lessons in painting. Bill joined the Masonic Lodge and the S. S. C. Club, a group of young men who kept it a secret that the initials stood for the Social Sardines Club.

At picnics, suppers, and dances he was most often attracted to lively, charming Caroline Eastman, known as Caddie to her friends. After several months they began planning for marriage and a home. But clubs, courting, or the cares of business never prevented Bill from following the national conflict through newspapers and letters from his brother Ed, now involved in some of the most bitter battles of the war.

Shortly before Christmas 1864, Mr. F. Styles, leading photographer of Burlington, offered Bill a position in his gallery at twenty-five dollars a week. That amount of money sounded like a fortune to Bill, and he knew he would learn a great deal about cameras and wet plates from Styles, who had an excellent reputation.

"But we'll never see each other," Caddie protested when Bill told her about the offer.

"Burlington is fairly close," Bill pointed out. "I could come to see you every Sunday. And we have to think about our future," he continued seriously.

"I counted on living in Rutland," Caddie objected. But in the end she reluctantly agreed.

Early in the spring of 1865, Bill moved to Burlington. Styles' Vermont Gallery, with its ornate chandelier hanging from the ceiling, oil paintings on the walls, and luxurious carpeting on the floor, seemed to Bill the height of elegance. Impressed by the well-furnished studio, excellent equipment, and the fine craftsmanship of his employer, he set to work with determination to become a master photographer.

Shortly before church time on Sunday, April 9, he was startled by a concerted, clamorous pealing of bells. Then he heard people running in the street outside the hotel where he had a room.

"The war is over!" someone shouted.

Ed would be coming home now, thought Bill, as he rushed outdoors to join the crowd that had appeared from nowhere. Men shouted, sang, and tooted on horns; some of the women cried. Among those with whom he touched elbows, Bill knew there were parents whose sons lay in shallow graves at Gettysburg or on some other battlefield. And what must it be like in the South, where homes, industries, railroads, and fields lay in ruins?

The following Saturday Bill stood with the same people in front of the telegraph station while they awaited news of President Lincoln, who had been shot by an assassin. He shared the shocked silence when the words flashed through, "The President is dead."

That winter Bill learned to play the flute and joined a literary society. He read Shakespeare and Dickens and mazazines such as *Harper's Weekly,* although the advertisements for pocket-size pistols, and Swamp Shrub Balsam guaranteed to grow a full beard, sometimes proved more fascinating than the articles. To keep himself in good physical condition, he exercised with Indian clubs and went sleighing on the glassy surface of Lake Champlain.

One Sunday in April 1866, Bill, as usual, took the train to Rutland to see Caddie. The year he had spent in Burlington had been a good one, he thought, as he heard the locomotive whistle for a crossing. At the studio, Styles often commended him on his work. He had found new friends, learned to enjoy books, and built his income to the point where he could entertain Caddie in style.

That afternoon while Bill and Caddie were riding in a buggy along a country road, a couple drove up alongside them. "Race you!" challenged the driver, a young man with a contemptuous expression.

Caddie put a restraining hand on Bill's arm, but a race seemed safe enough since no other vehicles were in sight. Bill forged ahead of the other driver, but then a wheel hit a rock on the road.

"Be careful!" screamed Caddie as the buggy lurched dangerously. Wanting to reassure her, Bill reined the horse to a stop.

"We would have won easily, if you hadn't gotten panicky," he accused on the way back to Caddie's home.

"You had no business racing," Caddie said hotly.

The argument grew into a full-fledged quarrel on matters aside from racing. A week later, Caddie broke the engagement.

Bill's satisfying little world had exploded in his face. He could think of nothing that would ease his heartache except flight. A few hours after he had told Mr. Styles that he could no longer work at the studio he boarded a train for New York City, although he had no idea what he would do there.

He couldn't be lonelier on a raft in the middle of the Atlantic, he thought as he got off the train. Weighted down by a heavy carpetbag, he set off on foot to find a hotel he could afford.

Next morning Bill wandered aimlessly up one street and down another. Around noon he saw a familiar figure striding toward him. "Rock!" he exclaimed, jubilant at seeing his friend Ruel Rounds of Company K.

"You hunting a good time or a job?" asked Rock, flicking a speck of lint off his shabby coat sleeve.

"I need to get work," Bill confided.

"Jobs are scarcer in New York than apple pie was in the Army," said Rock. "But I've heard that they need miners out in Montana territory. Why don't we try for a berth with a silver mining company that would pay our way out?"

At the end of the second day of haunting employment offices, Bill and Rock still had no offer. That night when they described their failure to Billy Crowl, a friend of Rock's, Crowl said, "I talked to a fellow today who just got back from Montana. There *are* jobs to be had once you get there."

"Why don't the three of us go on our own?" Rock jumped up and began pacing back and forth across Crowl's room.

"What would you say to pooling our cash and taking the train as far as we can?" suggested Crowl. "When we run out of money, we'll all get jobs and earn enough for the next leg of the trip."

"I'm flat broke," Rock confessed, "but I'll put in extra money later."

Bill reached for his wallet in the usual pocket. It was gone! His other pockets were equally empty and flat. "I—I must have lost my wallet," he said, swallowing dryly.

"Maybe you left it at the hotel," said Crowl.

"No, I know I had it. I guess you'll have to count me out," Bill went on, panicky at the thought that he didn't have money to pay his hotel bill or even to buy his next meal.

4: *More Hope than Cash*

THAT night, trying to decide what he should do next, Bill tossed on the bed and pommeled his pillow. Not until morning when he looked to see what time it was did an idea hit him. Why not hock his watch?

A pawnbroker gave him sixty-six dollars.

"With your cash added to mine we'll have railroad fare to Detroit," Crowl said. "My sister lives there—she might lend us enough to go on to Montana."

The trio left New York on a sunny April morning. As they rode westward on the hard benches of a second-class train, Caddie's face—serious, laughing, flirtatious—kept popping into Bill's mind. When the three young men reached Detroit, Crowl went to his sister's home. Bill and Rock, who had spent their last dime, walked dejectedly down a street rapidly whitening with snow.

"What are we going to do now?" asked Bill, pulling his coat collar up around his neck. "No cash. No chow. No bed."

Although embarrassed at the idea of begging for shelter, the adventurers spent the night on a mattress on the floor at the police station.

As they left the station next morning, Crowl swaggered toward them grinning confidently. "My brother-in-law came through with twenty dollars in hard cash," he told them. "Also this." He fished up a pass on the Michigan Central to Chicago.

"Where does that leave Bill and me?" asked Rock.

Crowl turned to Bill. "Of the three of us, you'd stand the best chance of finding a job in Chicago. I'll give you the pass and part of the money. Then—"

"Crowl and I can come later, hobo style," Rock broke in. "And you can feed us while we look for work."

In Chicago Bill found a job at a sign-painting studio, but left it after a short time to tutor a young man who wanted lessons in painting. He wrote to Rock and Crowl and some days later they arrived, half-starved, from Detroit. Over the meat, potatoes, and strawberries to which Bill treated them, they talked about the next move.

"A lot of wagon trains are made up at St. Joseph, Missouri," said Crowl. "Let's go there and get jobs as bullwhackers with an outfit headed for Montana."

Working as a teamster did not appeal to Bill, but then it occurred to him that in his spare time he might draw pictures of the trail as he had drawn camp life during the war. Sketches and landscapes ought to sell in the East. Perhaps he could do something even more important. The railroads, now pushing westward, would in another year or so bring an end to treks by covered wagons. Why couldn't he record for the future the land and lives of men who braved deserts, mountains, and tomahawk-brandishing Indians in their search for farms and fortunes?

As Bill's attention returned to his companions, he heard Crowl saying, "Of course we'd first have to earn enough money for railroad fare to St. Joseph."

Not until late in June did the trio, aboard a train with a wood-burning engine, arrive at the outskirts of St. Joseph. Here the railroad ended. Beyond lay the great West. Bill knew he'd soon be face to face with its peaks and perils.

Optimism wilted as he and his friends were turned away from one wagon depot after another. The depots were crowded with immigrants, ex-soldiers and adventurers, some of whom made rowdy remarks about the three Easterners still in the frock coats and stiff black hats they had worn at home. Finally at the Francis Street depot an official offered them jobs with a wagon train that would be leaving not from St. Joseph but from Nebraska City.

Thirst was the biggest problem on the boat the three friends had to take to get to Nebraska City.

"Ugh!" exclaimed Crowl after a drink from a pail of water drawn up out of the churning, yellowish Missouri River. "Liquid mud."

The hot sun beat down on the almost shadeless hurricane deck, turning their faces a fiery, painful red, and their throats were parched with the diet of cheese and crackers they had brought to eat on the trip.

In Nebraska City the trio hunted up their wagon boss Ed Owens, a tall, slightly stooped man with blond hair that hung down to his shoulders. He sent them to be outfitted at a store that smelled of tobacco and leather. There, the company agent issued each of them a rubber coat, a Colt revolver, cartridges, and other necessaries.

Before they left for their wagon camp outside Nebraska City, they all wrote home. Bill's family had not been impressed by his sign-painting job; what would they think of bullwhacking? He tried to describe the plan he had for sketching the life of the men who drove the covered wagons, but it was hard for him to put dreams into words.

After they had mailed their letters, the young men assembled their gear and hiked to the camp, where oxen bellowed and canvas-topped wagons stood ranged in a circle. A man named Frank, who identified himself as Owens' assistant, assigned each of them a wagon with two sections hitched together as a unit.

To Bill his wagon looked big and unwieldy. The thought of managing the oxen that would pull it so overwhelmed him that he hardly heard Frank say, "You'll be haulin' groceries for Virginia City."

At suppertime a lanky teamster with faded blue eyes, who introduced himself as Dan, showed them a quick way to make bread from the flour and baking soda that had been doled out to them. Then he demonstrated how to bake it in the Dutch oven.

"Any time there's somethin' that's a puzzle, just whistle," he told them. "I been trailin' a good many years."

"What puzzles me is how I'll yoke and drive twelve oxen." Crowl gestured helplessly.

"On the trail oxen are bulls," Dan corrected him. When the old-timer went on talking about yokes and chains his words made little sense to Bill, who became utterly confused about leaders, pointers, wheelers, and swing cattle. Eager to change the subject he asked, "What's the hardest thing about bullwhacking?"

Dan hesitated so long that Bill thought he wasn't going to answer, but finally he said quietly, "Distance—that's what makes men fall to pieces the most." Then as he started off toward his own wagon, Dan said, "Trailin' is hard work. Better hit your blankets early."

Dawn had just begun to splash pink on the slate-colored sky when an ear-splitting voice called, "Roll out."

A few minutes later several hundred half-wild bulls thundered into the corral formed by the circle of wagons. Boss Ed Owens, perched on the wheel of a wagon, pointed to the animals each teamster should take for his own use. After several hours of struggle, Bill, with help from Dan, managed to lasso and yoke the bulls assigned to him. But then he had trouble straightening out the heavy chains that ran from yoke to yoke.

At noon Owens gave the signal to roll. "Off to Montana!" whooped teamsters as they hurried to their wagons. Soon he would be in country where only a few men had been before him, Bill thought jubilantly. But by the end of the third hour out of Nebraska City his excitement had subsided. His muscles ached, his sunburn smarted, and his feet felt as if they were gripped in a vise.

The days after that all followed the same pattern. Owens got the bullwhackers up at dawn and, not stopping to eat breakfast, they drove from five o'clock to ten. Then, while the bulls grazed, the bullwhackers cooked a meal, greased wagons, or rested, and the yoking began all over again. Most of the experienced teamsters had such good control of their beasts that they could ride on the tongue of a wagon most of the time, but Bill had to walk and shoo his bulls. On the prairie, where grass stretched out like a limitless green sea, hot dry winds blew up choking clouds of dust. Bill's hands became calloused, his lips cracked. Sometimes he could get a refreshing drink of water from a stream, a spring, or a ranchhouse well, but frequently he had to try to satisfy his thirst with warm, flat-tasting water carried in a keg.

Bill reproached himself daily for having given up a promising career in Vermont. There, for doing a job he loved, he had been paid twenty-five dollars a week. Now, slaving at tasks that maddened him, he earned only twenty dollars a month.

As the wagon train moved westward, averaging only around fourteen miles a day, the ranches became fewer. Some had been abandoned because of the Indian menace. One day a rather large band of Otoe Indians appeared suddenly at the camp. Bill grabbed his revolver but felt foolish when Dan and other veteran bullwhackers began doling out harmonicas and beads. When he glanced toward Crowl's wagon, Bill saw an Indian sneaking away with a pound of tobacco. Alerted by the yell of a teamster, Crowl whipped out his Colt revolver and forced the Indian to return the tobacco. Immediately the braves vanished from the camp, but they looked sullen rather than pleased by their gifts.

As soon as the Otoes had ridden out of sight, Owens called a meeting. "Gentlemen," he drawled, "Indians in this country don't usually stop by just for a cup of tea. That's the reason you carry Colts and carbines." He paused and then said solemnly. "Never forget it. But," he added, looking sternly at Crowl, "don't use your guns unless you have to. Indians hold grudges, and out here there are more of them than there are of us."

From then on Bill noticed a difference in his trailmates. They watched the countryside like hawks with an air of expectancy, almost of grimness.

5: *Trials Trigger Tempers*

T HE BULLWHACKERS turned playful when on the evening of July 11 the adobe walls of Fort Kearny loomed to the west.

"Tomorrow," said a man who had joined Bill, Rock, and Crowl as a messmate, "we entertain ourselves inside the fort and forget bulls and Indians."

After their customary meal of bacon and bread that had come heavy as a bullet from the Dutch oven, Bill got out his flute, and Rock started singing:

> I'm a bullwhacker, far away from home.
> If you don't like me, just leave me alone.

One by one, trailmates drifted over to join in. Amid the music, jests, and hearty laughter it dawned on Bill that he no longer despised trailing. His sunburn had changed to tan, his muscles had toughened, and he had learned to handle the bulls. He had really become fond of them—especially Old Hickory and Stonewall. Almost every day he managed to do a little sketching.

Next morning as the train neared the stockade of pointed

76

logs, the prairie watered by the Platte River looked peaceful. But at the fort the bullwhackers heard sobering news. Because of Indian uprisings military officials would not permit any train of less than thirty wagons to travel beyond Fort Kearny. Owens had only twenty-five, so he joined forces with another train headed by a man named Doolittle.

West of the fort, the wagons rolled along a smooth, level road. At night the dust-begrimed bullwhackers could cool off in the Platte River. But neither the river nor the road offset the strain of unceasing vigilance, the monotony of driving the bulls hours on end, the endless struggle to keep wagons and bulls in good condition.

No two men reacted to trail life in the same way. Dan was always cheerful and helpful. But some never did their share of the cooking, hauling water, or rustling buffalo chips for fires, and they complained about everything from sowbelly to wages.

At California Crossing on the South Platte, Bill and his teammates worked two hours repacking their loads so anything that dampness might hurt would be above water level. Then they spent most of the rest of the day coaxing their bulls through quicksand and tricky currents and straining with their shoulders to the wheels to keep wagons from turning turtle.

Between fordings, Bill made hasty sketches of wagons, bullwhackers, and a band of half-naked Indian braves and their families. The Indian children waded into the water eagerly and then, followed by squaws leading pack ponies, paddled expertly to the opposite shore.

North of the California Crossing the rough terrain of the Scotts Bluff area, and the deep gullies and hairpin turns of the Mitchell's Pass Road slowed the train down so that it did not reach Fort Laramie until August 7. Behind the neat white-washed enclosure of adobe lay an almost self-sufficient settlement.

In the store redolent of cheese and dried herring, the sutler, with a diamond glittering in his shirt front, doled out mail to the bullwhackers. Bill took his handful of letters and went off to his wagon, where he could be alone to read them. His mother reported that his brothers all had jobs for the summer, except for young Allen, who constantly got into mischief and teased his tiny sister Emma.

"I feel sure Caddie would have you back," one friend had written. As Bill stood staring out over bleak sand hills, Caddie, the buggy rides, parties, seemed to him like part of a different world. He felt a sudden longing to be part of that world again, but he wouldn't want Vermont friends to see him as he was now. I won't go back until I'm rich or famous or both, he told himself fiercely.

Beyond Fort Laramie, sand and rocks made the going hard. Early one morning when the wagons were moving along a little beyond the Deer Creek Telegraph Station, a man galloped up shouting, "Indians!" He paused only long enough to explain breathlessly, "They fired the station and killed three of our men. I'm off to the military post up ahead to get help."

"Ready your carbines, men," Owens ordered abruptly.

A short time later the bullwhackers met several Army wagons filled with soldiers, but no Indians appeared.

Food shortages caused more tension than Indians. When the bacon turned rancid, Bill and Rock won the approval of their messmates by roasting sage hens and rabbits. But everyone complained when Owens stopped doling out sugar and molasses.

Rock and some of the others spooned out sugar for their coffee from the sacks in the cargoes of their wagons. After Owens caught several bullwhackers in the act, he assembled all the men and announced that the cost of the sugar taken would be deducted from their wages.

Angered by Owens' stinginess, Rock and a teamster named Gray left the train at the Sweetwater Station and got jobs cutting hay for horses owned by the telegraph company.

"Why don't you quit too?" Rock urged Bill. "Haying beats bullwhacking."

Bill was tempted, but he hated to leave Owens shorthanded. When the call came for the wagons to roll he said good-by to Rock, feeling that the trail had never looked longer or lonelier.

"Know how you feel," Dan said gruffly. "Havin' good mates shrinks the dangers of trailin'."

Good mates helped make chores more endurable too, thought Bill next day as he greased the wagon wheels by himself. The wagon train had made its noon stop at Independence Rock, a landmark on the Oregon Trail. Bill was on the last wheel when the Doolittle train stopped to exchange greetings and then went on.

With great interest Bill examined the warnings against Indians, records of distance, and initials scratched into the soft surface of the rock that looked like a huge, inert monster. Of what had the J.J.'s, the A.M.'s, and S.P.'s been dreaming, he wondered as he hastily scratched his own W.H.J.

Beyond Independence Rock in a gorge called Devil's Gate a severe thunderstorm made the bulls skittish. Next morning the train had been under way for only a short time when Bill saw the Doolittle wagons up ahead in a circle. They must be in trouble, he thought, or they would be on the trail by now.

Just then Owens rode up looking very solemn. "Lightnin' struck and killed one of their men," he said. "We'll join the crew for the buryin'."

Standing at the side of the grave, Bill remembered the young man as he had seen him yesterday. What had brought him on the trail? How sad that his life ended in this lonely place.

In the days that followed, Bill began to see what Dan had meant when he said distance was the hardest thing about trailing. It seemed that they traveled and traveled but got nowhere. Wagons broke down. So many bulls died that each driver had only ten left, and some of them were lame.

But trailing had its bright side too. On a cold night when the train corralled at an abandoned telegraph station, the bullwhackers found a number of pine logs and built a fire. Hunched up in front of the roaring flames that took the nip off a frost-edged wind, Bill felt a kind of closeness with his trailmates. He knew that Bill Maddern, who sat next to him was experiencing similar thoughts when he whacked him companionably.

Several days later, when the train stopped at the South Pass

Station to repair wagons, Bill talked to some soldiers about to be transferred East.

"Where you headed?" asked a dreamy-faced young man who looked more like a poet than a soldier.

"Virginia City," Bill told him.

The soldier frowned thoughtfully. "By the time you make it there it'll be winter, and you'll have to lay over until spring to get a wagon train out. Jobs are scarce up that way. If I were in your boots I'd drop out at Salt Lake City."

The conversation upset Bill. What if he got stranded in Virginia City with no job? Maybe he should leave the train at Salt Lake City and find work in a photographic studio. Bill had another jolt when he confided his newly formed plan to his messmates at suppertime.

"The way it looks now," said Crowl, "we won't get as far west as Salt Lake. There's a rumor that Owens will go north from Ham's Fork."

"If he does I have a notion to quit the train at the Fork and join a Mormon outfit bound for Salt Lake City." Bill set his cup down so hard that some of his coffee sloshed out onto the ground.

"I just might quit with you." Maddern bit savagely into his piece of tough bread. "Owens promised to go by way of Salt Lake. I don't like the way he says one thing and does another."

At the station at Ham's Fork on September 6, Bill found that his boss could hire teamsters to replace him and Maddern if they quit the train. That night, encamped at the Fork, the two

young men decided that if Owens announced his intention to
go north, they would pull out.

Before it was time to yoke their bulls the next morning,
the two conspirators walked over to where Owens stood talking
to Frank.

"Mr. Owens," said Bill, "we've been wondering if you still
plan to go by way of Salt Lake City."

Owens looked surprised. "Got any objections if we don't?"
he asked belligerently.

"W—well," said Bill, "we've heard jobs are scarce in Virginia
City, and—"

"Nothin' but rumors." Owens anchored his hat more firmly
on his head. "We're rollin' north. Now."

"Not me," said Bill.

"I'll leave the train too," added Maddern.

"Why you—" Owens said. "You have to go on. You're
under contract."

"We didn't sign a thing," Bill reminded him.

"You were outfitted by the company," said Owens, livid
with anger. "And—"

"We'll turn back everything that isn't ours," Maddern told
him. When Frank unleashed a series of blistering curses, Bill
turned toward his wagon. He regretted that his decision had
stirred up so much ill will, but it didn't seem right for him to
go on.

It took only a few minutes to sort out the items the company
had issued and to say good-by to Crowl and Dan.

"You get busy now with your sketchin' pencils and

cameras," Dan told him. "Trailin' is in my blood, but you got somethin' better to do."

"Ready?" asked Maddern.

Bill picked up his carpetbag. When he and Maddern passed their bulls, as yet unyoked, Bill stopped to give Stonewall a pat. Who would be driving him today?

A little way from camp, Bill stopped to look back at the circle of canvas-covered wagons. Since June they had been the only home he had known. At times his trailmates had been boring, lazy, or hot-tempered, but when danger threatened they had all pulled together. Would he ever see any of them again?

6: *False Moves*

WHILE waiting for a westbound wagon train, Bill and Maddern worked at a haying camp. Late in September they signed as bullwhackers with an outfit headed for Salt Lake City.

In Parley's Park, mid-October suddenly turned to midwinter. Wagons mired down in the knee-deep snow mixed with mud that sucked and gurgled under the feet of the oxen. Bill had no warm clothing and the cold pierced to his bones. His misery increased when the soles came off his moccasins, but he still took his turn at night herding.

Next morning his feet were so swollen and sore that he had to stay in the lurching wagon that jolted and bruised his body. All the discomforts of the trail would not matter, he thought, if only he could succeed in painting pictures that would make people really sense the vast beauty of the West, the tenacity and courage of men going into the unknown. He reached for his sketchbook. It wasn't where he usually kept it. As he rummaged around frantically, he tried to think where he had last used it.

Finally he had to accept the fact that it had been left be-

hind some place on the trail. All his fine dreams about painting the West amounted to exactly nothing at this point, he told
himself bitterly.

After two days of inactivity, Bill could drive his bulls again.
When he stood on a crest looking down upon the emerald-
green foliage of Salt Lake City, circled by snowy peaks, he
forgot the hardships of the journey.

At the outskirts of the town, the wagons passed abruptly
from sagebrush and greasewood to a broad street lined with
young locust and cottonwood trees. Late autumn flowers gave
color, and the trees that surrounded almost every house
drooped with loads of peaches and apples.

"Yippee, we've rolled the miles!" shouted one of the bullwhackers.

As others took up the cry, children burst out of houses along
the street. Women followed with aprons full of fruit.

Bill stammered with embarrassment as he thanked a pretty
young woman for some peaches. She must find his appearance
revolting, he thought. From his shaggy hair and beard to the
tip of the rundown boots given to him by a fellow bullwhacker,
he felt dirty and disreputable.

Unable to find a furnished room they could afford, Bill and
Maddern rented an empty one and equipped it with a table,
a sheet-iron stove, and blocks of wood for chairs. They slept
in blankets on the floor and cooked in a skillet used on the
trail.

As Bill set off to hunt a job, he enjoyed the novelty of being
in the "City of the Saints." There were constant reminders of
Mormonism—the Temple with its wooden dome; the store-

house to which every Mormon donated a tenth of his income in money, pigs, hay, or molasses. Everywhere the beehive coat-of-arms was visible to symbolize industry.

No paint shop or photographic studio wanted Bill's services. The money he had earned from bullwhacking didn't buy much when prices were so high—even potatoes cost a dollar a bushel. The day came when he had only a few pennies left.

He and Maddern finally got jobs on a farm four miles out of the city, owned by a stooped, kindly man named Birch. Bill hauled bricks for a new barn, made portraits of the Birch family, entertained the children, and whittled chessmen. While Maddern blasted away on a trumpet, Bill played his flute. In the evenings they sat in the kitchen playing games or reading aloud to the family, none of whom could read or write.

After Bill had written a long letter to his family one day, he had an impulse to write to Caddie as well, for he fancied himself still in love with her. She never replied to his letter, but the writing of it plunged him into a period of self-questioning. Life was pleasant at the Birches, but what was he accomplishing that would be of lasting value?

Maddern too became restless. "Let's head for California with a wagon train," he urged.

Already homesick, Bill didn't want to go a step farther west, but he kept thinking about the good job opportunities in California that Birch's father-in-law had told about. "I'll go," he finally told Maddern, "but not as a bullwhacker. I want to paint instead of coaxing bulls along the trail."

He and Maddern signed as passengers on a wagon train managed by Ed Webb that was slated to leave around December 21, and Bill spent all he could afford on drawing and painting equipment.

Not until they were saying good-by did Bill realize how fond he had become of the Birches. After their farewell to the rest of the family, Mr. Birch followed Bill and Maddern outside and handed a bulky parcel to each of them. "A few extra victuals for the trail," he said.

"Thank you. Thank you for all your kindness," said Bill, feeling that the words did not at all say what he wanted them to say.

"Don't thank me for nothin'," Birch told him. "There's only one thing I wish you'd leave with me, and that's your learnin'."

I've been the learner, thought Bill. He wished he had the patience and simple kindness of these people he would probably never see again. As he and Maddern turned and started down the road leading into Salt Lake City, Bill seemed to hear above the cadence of their boots, Good-by, good-by. Only a little over three months ago, he had parted with wise old Dan and his other trailmates. Life had become a series of good-bys.

Bill's spirits spiraled upward when he and Maddern got within sight of the Webb encampment. How often he and his brother Ed had talked about seeing the far West!

As the train of mule-drawn wagons traveled southward through small Mormon settlements, Bill spent much of his time sketching hills with strong shadows and blue skies with fleecy white clouds. If he hadn't finished a picture by the time Ed Webb gave orders to roll, he stayed behind and caught up by noon or nightfall. While with the Owens outfit, he'd had to satisfy himself with crude sketches. Now he worked hard to perfect his drawing and painting.

Maddern teased him about his passion for accuracy the day he found him counting the spokes on a wagon wheel. "What difference does it make?" he asked. "It's only a painting."

Bill grinned and said nothing. How could he explain that he wanted to capture the exact truth?

Life was much less rugged than it had been on the two previous wagon trains. Chores, which he need not have taken on at all because he was a paying passenger, seemed no burden at all when shared with Maddern and two other messmates, Sergeant and Gibbons, who did their part with speed and good humor. The cook, known as Uncle Billy, prepared appetizing stews and sauces. In the evening when all the teamsters got together, Mrs. Webb, wife of the wagon boss, sometimes sang Scottish songs. Bill played his flute, and Uncle Billy earned cheers by dancing a double hornpipe.

But there were bad times too. Steep climbs and descents taxed men and mules. After the train reached the Mojave Desert in January, searing winds like blasts from an oven blew up blinding, stinging sandstorms. Heat from the soil scorched the soles of Bill's shoes, and often there was no water to slake the burning thirst.

The Webb train reached Los Angeles on the last day of January. Tile-roofed houses and birds chorusing in the palms made the city of five thousand people seem very gay and colorful compared to sober, winter-bound Salt Lake City. Bill and Maddern had planned to find jobs in Los Angeles, but their messmates urged them to go to San Francisco and get jobs in a mining area.

"You'll earn money faster for passage East," Sergeant pointed out. "You might even make a fortune."

Another trailmate advised Bill and Maddern to work their way north to the Clear Creek mines. "There are ranches all along the road," he told them. "You could get jobs at any of them."

Fortified by crackers and cheese, they set off. By the third night the vagabonds still had no jobs. To escape the clammy chill of oncoming darkness, they took refuge in a haymow. Bill disliked spending the night in a barn like some tramp. Was he becoming an aimless wanderer? he asked himself. After the quarrel with Caddie, it had seemed that going miles away from her would solve his problems. Now he realized they could never be solved except by honest thinking. Somehow he must conquer the restlessness that had lured him from place to place with promises that were never fulfilled. From now on he was through with false moves. He would take the first job he could find, earn money for passage East, and begin his career as a photographer.

The next afternoon, at Twenty Mile Ranch, a stagecoach stop at the entrance to the San Joaquin Valley, the pleasant-faced proprietor, D. Ward, offered him and Maddern jobs as hired men.

Bill wanted to stay, but Maddern said, "I'm going on. Mining sounds more exciting than milking cows and digging irrigation ditches."

It bothered Bill to have his friend starting off with no cash.

"Here," he said, pulling out a cheap watch he had bought
in Salt Lake City. "Take this. It isn't worth much, but you
could raise a little money with it."

In Maddern's eyes Bill saw more gratitude than could be
spoken. In an attempt at gaiety Maddern quipped, "I'll bring
your watch back as soon as I've dug up a fortune." Then he
wheeled and walked off down the road. For months they had
shared danger, decisions and hopes, and now Bill was alone
among strangers with whom he could talk only about things
that meant the least to him.

Bill worked hard digging irrigation ditches, and carrying
water, carpetbags, and fuel to the rooms of stagecoach
guests. In his spare time he shot arrows at targets he and
Ward's son Nels set up, and painted landscapes that his boss
wanted for the guest rooms.

By the end of March, Bill had enough cash to go to Los
Angeles and arrange for transportation home. He planned to
work his way as far as the Mississippi River and then use the
money he'd saved to buy a ticket on a passenger train to
Vermont.

In Los Angeles his former wagon boss Ed Webb suggested
that Bill might get a job with an outfit driving horses to
Omaha. The boss, he explained, bought cheap horses or
rounded up wild ones and sold them for fancy prices.

Sam McGannigan, who owned the horses, hired Bill but
warned that the outfit would not be leaving for a few days.
Days ran into weeks. Bill worried at the way meals and room
rent made his cash dwindle. When the long delay brought
Bill to the end of his savings, McGannigan asked him to move

out to the horse camp to help lasso, herd, water, shoe, and brand the half-wild horses and tough little mustangs which were to be driven to Omaha.

On the morning of May 3, McGannigan gave orders to be ready to leave by noon. Elation bubbled within Bill as, astride a bald-faced bay, he followed the herd of one hundred and fifty horses. Near San Gabriel Mission another outfit, herding three hundred horses, joined the McGannigan crew of four. Jim Kellar, the grizzled boss, had with him his wife and three herders.

Herding horses was the hardest work Bill had ever done. On the desert, both herders and horses became frantic from the glare of the white sand and lack of water. Sometimes the horses stampeded. Sam raved and ranted continually. To ease the monotony of their rugged routines, Bill and Jim Begole, a young man from Michigan, watched for peculiarities in behavior of their animals and named them accordingly—Lummox, Granny, Satan.

As days passed with no free time for sketching or painting, Bill fretted over the postponement of his career. He tried to console himself with the thought that for the first time in over a year he was traveling eastward instead of westward. But he could not quite free himself from the fear that he might be making another one of those false moves he had promised himself he would avoid.

Gorsline

7: Cameraman for Merchants and Chiefs

BACK IN Mormon country in early June, Bill saw many familiar landmarks. At Salt Lake City, Johnnie, who had been driving the supply wagon, left to go home, and Sam assigned Bill to the job. Except for the jolting and jouncing, handling it was easier than herding.

"I wish Sam would hire more herders," Jim Kellar said rebelliously the day a wagon train passed their camp east of Salt Lake City and the wagon master warned them that it was folly to be traveling in Indian country with a crew of only seven men.

"I do too," Bill agreed. "In the Owens and Webb trains we

had a much larger crew; and when we corralled, the wagons shielded us."

Next day McGannigan and Kellar quarreled violently. Finally the enraged Kellar shouted, "I'm clearin' out with my horses and my herders."

That leaves three of us, Bill thought grimly as he watched Kellar's party receding into the distance. Three men against hundreds of hostile Indians.

Fort Bridger, where wild roses and willow trees grew outside the high walls, offered a welcome relief from the barren, dangerous country the herders had just traversed. But beyond the fort everything went wrong. Rumors about horse thieves in the area meant redoubled watchfulness. Mosquitoes attacked in armies. The horses, whether irritated by the insects or by some other cause, stampeded at intervals. The herders lost sleep rounding them up.

Sam raged and ranted. It was hard to tell whether the men or the horses were wildest, Bill thought one day as he tried to coax the terrified animals across a flooded stream.

Toward the end of July, Bill kept seeing signs that the Union Pacific Railway was making a determined push westward. Pawnees, hired by the United States government and armed with both guns and tomahawks, guarded construction workers.

At Julesburg, Sam announced that he would ship the horses by rail to Omaha. Bill looked forward to relaxing in a seat on the train; but after the last animal was loaded, Sam said bluntly, "You and Jim can hop on that flatcar."

On the second night of the journey, the two herders, who

had shivered in the prairie breeze the night before, got a blanket and climbed into a boxcar. The floor strewn with kernels of corn made a poor bed, but Bill tried to forget discomfort by concentrating on plans for the future. Many of the experiences he'd undergone had given him a new maturity, but would Vermont friends look upon him as a kind of tramp?

At Omaha, Bill helped Sam set up the horse camp on miry bottom land two miles outside of town. Then, eager to begin the trip to Vermont, he asked for his pay. Sam kept stalling and insisted that he stay a while longer. After three days of excuses and delays, Sam finally handed him a bill.

"But this is only twenty dollars!" Bill protested.

"That's all the trip is worth." Sam's mouth shut in a hard, straight line.

"Look, Sam," said Bill, "counting the time at the horse camp, I worked for you almost four months. And twenty dollars won't begin to buy a ticket East and the new suit of clothes I'll have to have." He looked down in distaste at his filthy trousers.

"It'll be easy to earn your fare home," Sam told him. "You can stay at the camp while you're looking around for a job in Omaha."

Bill bristled, but when he saw Sam's fingers curl menacingly around the revolver in his belt, he knew it would be useless to argue. Turning away, he walked off toward town. Twenty dollars, he thought bitterly, for enduring Sam's surliness, the blistering heat of the desert, the drenchings in swollen creeks, the lonely vigils under the stars. He had planned to leave for home a few hours after he reached Omaha. Now he might be stranded for weeks.

The suit that Bill had to buy before he could go job hunting took most of the twenty dollars Sam had paid him. He spent the rest for a shave. From the barber he got the addresses of two photographic studios. At the second one, kindly, middle-aged Mr. Hamilton offered him a job for fifteen dollars a week. "I'll increase your salary to twenty-five dollars," he said, "if your products are good."

They'd be good, thought Bill, as he left the studio to look for a room. All he had learned from Mowrey and Styles would soon come back to him, and he'd work hard to improve. A new sense of purpose and steadiness welled up in him. No longer was he Bill the herder of horses, but W. H. Jackson, photographer.

Mr. Hamilton soon showed his confidence in him by letting him take over the management of a branch studio on a share basis. He couldn't ask for a more considerate, congenial boss, thought Jackson, but he didn't want to work much longer in anyone else's studio; he wanted his own.

Since he already had a foothold in Omaha, it seemed best to stay there instead of starting over again in Vermont. Anyway, he liked the bustling town and friendly people.

To save money to invest in a business of his own, he lived almost as frugally as he had on the trail. The chance for ownership came sooner than he expected. Mr. Hamilton, who wanted to return to his farm in Iowa, offered to accept a reasonable down payment and let Jackson pay the rest out of earnings. Bill's father, when Bill wrote to him about the ar-

rangement, volunteered to put up the entire sum owed to
Hamilton, if Bill would take his brothers into the business. Bill
agreed eagerly, and very soon Fred and Ed arrived in Omaha
to work with him.

Ed, who had had experience as a bookkeeper, handled ac-
counts and managed the office and advertising. Although Fred
was only seventeen and had the handicap of deafness, he became a capable assistant. Railroad men, farmers, townspeople
flocked to the Jackson Brothers Studio. Ira Johnson, a boyhood
friend of Bill's from Troy, came to handle most of the portrait
work. Bill did outside jobs—photographing shop fronts and
farms, and groups of club and lodge members.

Occasionally an Indian from one of the reservations in the
vicinity of Omaha showed up in the waiting room. One day
an Omaha who spoke English confided to Jackson, "On the
rails will come many settlers. Will push Indians off the land
of their fathers."

Even if the settlers didn't take the Indians' land, they would
change the Indians' way of living, thought Jackson. He didn't
suppose he could do much about helping them keep old customs; such action might not even be wise. But he could visit
the reservations and take pictures of wickiups, costumes,
customs, and ceremonies of a vanishing way of life. Such
photographs would be valuable to historians, museum staffs,
and anthropologists in the future.

Bill, Ed, and Ira built a portable darkroom so that he could
visit reservations for three or four days at a time. In the small
shack mounted on the running gear of a light buggy, they in-
stalled a tank for clear water, a sink for developing, and odds

and ends of equipment including the various chemicals neces-
sary in wet-plate photography.

For his first trip to a reservation, Jackson settled himself
in front of his horse-drawn darkroom and drove off in high
spirits. But the venture failed to meet his expectation. When
he asked permission to take pictures, many Indians glowered
at him and muttered, "Bad medicine."

But a few consented when he offered them knives, tobacco,
cash, or clothing. The Indians would be less camera shy next
time, Jackson told himself hopefully. By then they would see
that no great evil had befallen those who had been photographed, and others would be more willing to pose. Return he
must. The filth and squalor he had seen had shocked him.
Through pictures he meant to dramatize what reservation life
had done to a once free people.

Eventually Jackson convinced the Indians that he had a
friendly purpose in his picture making. "We like you because
you see us as persons," one Indian leader told him.

Soon, heralded as the man-with-the-magic-eye, Jackson
found a welcome wherever he went. Otoe, Osage, and Ponca
braves posed for him in everything from loin cloths to costumes bedecked with beads, bells, or cheap medals. Pawnee
chief Peta-la-sha-ra wore an elaborate feather headdress reaching almost to the ground. Indian women, often too shy to sit
for a portrait, allowed Jackson to take their pictures while
they stretched buffalo skins, did beadwork, or prepared meals
over a campfire.

Jackson had no training in chemistry, but he understood
the principles involved in mixing developing solutions, and his

skill contributed to the excellence of his photographs. Sometimes he experimented with a stereo camera, from which he could turn out prints with two pictures taken at slightly different angles. When viewed through the specially designed glass eyepieces of a stereoscope, the pictures fused and gave a three-dimensional effect. After the pictures and stereographs had a good sale through local outlets, Ed sent a number of them East.

Although Bill spent most of his time with cameras, he made many new friends in Omaha. At the home of the John Campbells, he met Mollie Greer, who had come from Warren, Ohio, for a visit. Very attractive in a quiet way, she listened with intelligent interest when he talked about photography. Bill found great satisfaction in her companionship, and soon he was deeply in love.

After a short engagement, Mollie and Bill set their wedding date for May 10, 1869. A few days before the event, an official of a stereograph company came to the studio. "Would you," he asked Jackson, "be interested in making stereographic scenes along the new Union Pacific right-of-way this summer? We'd like to have Easterners who use stereoscopes in their parlors get some idea of what the West is like."

Photography of colorful sandstone cliffs and sculptured buttes appealed to Jackson, but he had to think about Mollie.

"I don't know," he said. "You see, I'm about to be married, and I don't suppose there'd be living accommodations out that way for a lady. And—well, there's the question of finances, too."

"We'd pay a modest sum for up to ten thousand pictures,"

the official told him. "Food would be free if you ate with maintenance crews, and the Union Pacific would give you passes."

The prospect of riding the railroad made Jackson's pulse quicken. Since his days on the trail his imagination had been captured by the thrust of locomotives into the wilderness. At this very moment tie-cutting and spike-driving construction crews of rival railroads were pushing toward a meeting place in Utah Territory.

"I'll talk it over with Mollie and let you know," Jackson promised.

"This could mean a lot to your reputation," the stereo representative said as he left the studio. "Stereographers would convince viewers all over the country that the imprint of W. H. Jackson means quality."

Jackson knew this would be his chance to establish himself as a front-rank scenic photographer. But he couldn't let Mollie eat with railroad crews and sleep in a tent. Neither could he bear to think about leaving her in Omaha for the summer. Perhaps someone else's camera would be the first to record the cliffs, peaks, and lonely rocks along the new railroad.

Gotslinc

8: *Biographer of Rocks and Lonely Places*

BEFORE Bill had finished telling about the offer to photograph the right-of-way along the Union Pacific, Mollie said, "We have to think about your career."

"I don't care so much about the publicity," said Jackson. "I do care about giving people pictures of the beauty out here in the West and making them realize what it has taken to build a transcontinental railroad. Why, I saw the Union Pacific when crews putting down rails had to be ready at any minute to swap shovels for guns!"

Mollie grasped his arm understandingly. "Your pictures could capture what you've just said for people both now and in the future."

Later, she and Bill agreed that Ed could manage the studio. Mollie would go to her family in Ohio after the wedding.

"But we'll sandwich in a honeymoon first," Jackson insisted.

He had never been happier than at high noon on May 10, 1869, when, with Mollie standing slender and graceful beside him, he heard Bishop Clarkson pronounce them man and wife. Shortly after the ceremony they boarded a Missouri River steamer. Passengers were talking excitedly about the joining of the railroads which had taken place that day. Leland Stanford, President of the Central Pacific, had driven a solid gold spike connecting that railroad with the Union Pacific at Promontory Point, Utah Territory. Jackson was thinking of another linkage—of his life and Mollie's.

As the steamer floated slowly down the Missouri River, the terrible restlessness that had gripped him ever since he could remember drained away. After six days of happy companionship, the honeymooners disembarked at St. Louis, where Mollie boarded a train for Ohio. Jackson stood watching until he could no longer see her handkerchief fluttering from the car window.

On the way back to Omaha, he tried to offset his loneliness

by concentrating on plans for his summer work. As an assistant
he had chosen a photographer named Hull, a good cameraman
and a steady worker. The biggest problem would be trans-
porting equipment. Jackson would have to take two cameras—
one a standard 8-by-10-inch and the other a stereo. Besides
the cameras there would be a tripod, fragile glass plates, and
chemicals.

On June 23, Jackson and Hull reached Cheyenne, a noisy,
wooden-front town which had sprung up as result of railroad
construction. Jackson was surprised when a bearded man with
a scholarly bearing unlike the gamblers and brawling traders
who frequented the street came up to him and said, "You're
W. H. Jackson, aren't you?"

"Yes, I am," Jackson replied, but—"

"I'm Hayden." The stranger introduced himself. "I'm here
on a reconnaissance mission for the United States Geological
Survey. I've seen some of your photographs. They strike me as
outstanding."

Jackson was pleased at this high praise from a man of
Hayden's caliber. Dr. Ferdinand Vandeveer Hayden, a professor at the University of Pennsylvania, had won recognition
as a geologist and explorer. During their brief conversation,
Jackson got a very favorable impression of Hayden's energy
and enthusiasm.

After leaving Cheyenne by train, Jackson and Hull worked
in the Weber Canyon area in Utah Territory. To get to scenery
some distance from the tracks, the two photographers had to
walk and lug their heavy camping and photographic gear.

For Jackson, this was the beginning of a period of experimentation in capturing landscapes at different times of day and in different moods. The wet-plate process of photography was difficult at best. Now in an outdoor studio, procedures became even more complicated. To prepare a clean plate for exposure, Jackson balanced it on the thumb and forefinger of his left hand. Then he poured the sirupy collodion on the left-hand corner and worked the thick fluid around the edges and all over the plate. He became so adroit at this that he rarely had one excess drop, but wind-blown dust sometimes settled on the plate before he got it coated. Before loading the wet plate into the camera, Jackson dipped it in a bath of nitrate of silver.

When he had taken a photograph, and while the plate was still wet, he rushed it to the darkroom which he had improvised from the box in which he and Hull carried their photographic equipment. Over the box he had erected a folding frame with a hood of black and yellow calico. Working in a kneeling position under the hood, he developed the latent image with iron sulphate and fixed it with cyanide of potassium solution.

Jackson rinsed the plate in water. If the negative turned out well he placed the plate in a grooved plate box as soon as it had dried. Many times the image came out overexposed or underexposed because of a poor guess in timing. When such a failure occurred, Jackson corrected it immediately by making another exposure.

No matter where the photographers pitched their tent they followed much the same routine. Food varied with location. In isolated areas where the partners had to pack in supplies they lived on bread, bacon, and coffee. When close to a Union

Pacific section house they shared beans and prunes with crews whose motto, Jackson wrote to Mollie, seemed to be "Work, drink, and fight."

Workmen often gave the two men a lift on their handcars, and obliging engineers stopped whenever the photographers flagged them. One day, however, a new engineer, unaware of the arrangement, steamed past, leaving them in a cloud of smoke and cinders. At first, Jackson both tired and hungry, could think only of his disappointment. Then he looked at Hull, unshaven and unkempt, and began to laugh. "Guess the engineer thought we were a couple of tramps," he said cheerfully. "Can't say that I blame him."

In the vicinity of Corinne in Utah Territory the weather turned hot and windy. "Nice landscape, if you could see it," Hull said one morning as swirls of sand stung their eyes and filtered into blankets, food, and photographic equipment. Even when the wind died down a yellowish haze in the air made photography impossible. That evening the partners went into Corinne for a meal at Uinta House. There they met a photographer named Crissman, who allowed them to use his studio while they were in the vicinity.

Several times during the summer, Jackson went by stagecoach to Salt Lake City to buy photographic supplies. For relaxation after his business had been accomplished, he swam at Warm Springs and then settled down at Salt Lake House to read while he nibbled on fresh fruit.

"I'm soaking up enough entertainment to last for the next session in the wilderness," he wrote to Mollie after he attended a play at the elegant show house with carved, gilded stage boxes.

Back in rugged country in eastern Utah, Jackson and Hull endured wind, dust, and almost constant thirst. But despite hardships, Jackson was enthusiastic about his work. Sometimes it seemed to him that everything that had happened in his life had been preparing him to become a pictorial biographer of this mighty land. He did wish, though, that he had a camera that would record the reds and greens of the spectacular rock formations worn by wind, water, and weather. At night, lying exhausted on a blanket on the ground and surrounded by silence and stars, Jackson would think about Mollie and their plans for the future.

Late in September, Jackson rode into the Uinta mountains with a small group of men acquainted with the area. He interspersed hours of photography with fishing and hunting for ducks and sage hens.

When the season's work was over and Jackson was on the train bound for Omaha he reviewed in his mind what he had accomplished. People who viewed his stereographs would see the natural wonders of Devil's Slide, Hanging Rock, and other scenes never before recorded on a camera. And the photographs of blacksmiths and gamblers in Cheyenne, of railroad crews along the right-of-way, would give Easterners an idea of the character of the new frontier and the thrust of restless men in search of adventure.

Back in Omaha, Bill helped Mollie arrange furniture in their living quarters above the Jackson gallery. That winter, 1869–1870, Mollie learned so much about photography that she became a real asset in the studio. But the Jackson Brothers, for the first time since they had bought the business, had to woo customers. Mismanagement of finances by railroad magnates and shaky federal finances had brought on a national depression.

On a hot day in July 1870, Jackson, sorting supplies in a back room at the gallery, heard the bell on the street door announce a visitor. Hurrying into the waiting room, he was surprised to see the dynamic Dr. Hayden, whom he had met in Cheyenne the previous summer.

"I had a stopover on my way to an assignment in Wyoming," Hayden explained. "Decided to drop in and see how your pictures from last summer turned out."

After Jackson handed him a folio, the geologist looked long and earnestly at a photograph of rock formations. "I have trouble justifying my Survey work," he said with a sigh. "Congressmen glance through reports and promptly forget them. But if they had pictures like these . . ."

"Photographs do sometimes speak more loudly than words," Jackson agreed.

"They would help on the conservation aspect too," Hayden continued as he sat studying a Uinta mountain scene. "If lawmakers could grasp the majesty of the country, they might be more alert in keeping out private interests that pollute streams and wreck the forests." Hayden handed back the folio, sat silent for a moment, and then said, "I wish I could offer enough to make it worth your while to go along with the Survey party."

"What *could* you offer?" asked Jackson, already captivated

at the idea of using photography in the interests of conservation.

"Little more than your keep," said Hayden.

Jackson shook his head regretfully. "That would be ample, if I were a bachelor like you. But I have a fairly new business and also a new wife."

Just then Mollie entered the studio. "Excuse me," she apologized, starting to withdraw.

"Don't leave," said Hayden, who went on to introduce himself. "I've been telling your husband how much I'd like to take him with me to help with the Survey, but he prefers your company."

"There's more to it than that," Mollie replied. "It is all very well to take a summer off now and then, but he has a studio to maintain, and—"

"True," said Hayden, "but I can't help wondering if he wouldn't be serving the cause of photography and his nation better if he participated in the Survey."

Mollie looked at Dr. Hayden for a moment, then at Bill. Then she smiled. The smile told Jackson that she understood and that she wanted him to go.

"I could manage the business," Mollie said calmly.

Jackson fingered his watch chain nervously. His brother Ed, who had taken charge the preceding summer, had married and gone to live on his father-in-law's farm near Blair, Nebraska. "I know you could do it," he told Mollie, "but it would be too much to ask."

"Not when it would help you."

Seeing the wholehearted sincerity in Mollie's eyes, Jackson knew she meant what she said. What a wise, unselfish woman she was, he thought gratefully. "I'll go," he said, turning to Hayden.

Acceptance of the Hayden invitation meant that Jackson would be one of the first photographers to use his craft in the service of science. To win support for the Survey and for conservation he would put all the skill he had into his photography. Eager to begin his work, Jackson could hardly wait to pack his camera and chemicals.

9: *Picture-Maker For Uncle Sam*

JACKSON was impressed by the character and capabilities of the group Hayden had assembled at Camp Carlin, two miles out of Cheyenne. Besides geologists, it included Cyrus Thomas, a distinguished ethnologist, and the prominent artist Sanford Robinson Gifford.

"Exactly how will my photography fit in?" asked Jackson after Hayden had told him that besides surveying and making maps of lands, water, and minerals, he expected to secure information on geology and plant life.

"I'll want pictures of our party doing assigned tasks, but I'll also want pictures of the terrain, vegetation, and scenery." Hayden's face lighted up with expectation. "If we can convince Congress of the importance of wise use of this land and its resources, the Survey will be worth many times what it will cost the government."

On the morning of August 7, 1870, the date set for the Hayden expedition to start, rain slanted down in long, gray lines. But Jackson and the other men in the party, which now numbered twenty counting teamsters, voted to go ahead. Jackson carefully packed his chemicals and a supply of glass plates in two brightly painted rawhide saddlebags. These he hung by the loops over the pack saddle of the fat little mule assigned to him. "It's a big load, Hypo, but you can tote it," he said encouragingly as he lashed on a tripod and a keg of water for washing photographic plates.

The four heavy, mule-drawn wagons carrying supplies and camping equipment lumbered off followed by men on horseback. Jackson rode a cavalry mount up Lodge Pole Creek, where he had once walked as a bullwhacker.

Each morning, after breakfast and an informal conference, the men split up into teams. While some of the geologists surveyed or mapped the region, others collected rock specimens and fossils or calculated the flow of a stream. Sometimes Jackson made a side trip with only Hypo for company. On one such excursion he photographed a hitherto unmapped canyon.

"The next map of the region I send to Washington will include this canyon," Hayden promised. "Since you discovered it, I'll name it Jackson Canyon."

Jackson had never worked longer hours, but his activities engrossed him. Hayden's continued appreciation of his photographic efforts inspired him to give his best.

Almost every night after a satisfying meal prepared by their chef, John Raymond, the party sang. John could be dour and crotchety, but he mellowed when he had a guitar in his hands and he led the music with gusto. Members of the Survey talked a great deal about their individual projects but always in a spirit of cooperation rather than competition.

At Fort Laramie, mail awaited Jackson. He read Mollie's letter first. Her concern warmed him but made him lonely for the sound of her voice. The letter from his mother said the house still seemed empty with Bill, Ed, Fred, and Mary Elizabeth all gone. "But Allen and Emma are lively and active," she added. Some time soon he must take Mollie East and get reacquainted with his family, Jackson thought wistfully.

From Fort Laramie the Survey party worked up the Platte and Sweetwater rivers toward South Pass. Near Camp Stambaugh, a post on the crest of the divide, Jackson saw an encampment of Shoshone Indians.

"I'd like to get pictures of them," he said to Hayden, who had come up beside him, "but I suppose they wouldn't fit in with the purposes of your Survey."

"Oh, but they would." Hayden's voice was enthusiastic. "Photographs of their way of life might help in shaping reservation policies."

Chief Washakie, tall and looking every inch a hunter, greeted Jackson courteously in English and agreed to pose. But as soon as he knew the camera was focused on him he froze with the keep-out look Jackson had seen on the faces of so many Indians around Omaha. Trying to encourage the Chief to reveal something of his true character, Jackson led him to talk about the Shoshones. As the chief told about their customs, his face reflected alertness and concern for his people. "They have so little except their land," he said. "But the earth gives them beaver, antelope, sage hens, and herbs."

Later, walking among the lodges, Jackson photographed Shoshone women smoking fish, doing beadwork, weaving baskets, making soup, and spreading roots out to dry. While boys with bows shot arrows at targets, little girls played with buckskin dolls tied on tiny cradleboards.

After the Survey party left Camp Stambaugh and arrived on the sandy wastes between South Pass and Green River, heat sapped Jackson's energy. Wind and dust hampered his photography. Hayden, intense and nervous, at times made unreasonable demands, but Jackson realized that the high goals he had set for the Survey and for himself accounted for his exacting requirements.

For a trip into the Uinta mountains, genial Judge Carpenter, who made his home at Fort Bridger, acted as guide. The spare man with flaxen hair and beard guided geologists to valuable finds and assisted the cook in providing plentiful supplies of deer, elk, and trout.

One night, John Raymond, who had not taken into account the effect of altitude on the boiling point of water, served potatoes that could hardly be pierced by a fork. "Never saw such gosh-awful hard spuds," he complained. From that night on, Jackson and the others called their cook Potato John.

As Jackson photographed forests, streams, and wildlife in the Uintas he realized that the West was bigger and more impressive than most Americans knew. He longed for his pictures to make people aware of it, rouse them to protect its greatness.

After the expedition to the Uintas, the party proceeded southeast to Fort Sanders, where they were to disband. As he was packing his supplies for shipment to Omaha, Jackson was thinking that except for his eagerness to see Mollie he was reluctant to have the trip end. He had never known finer companionship. He turned around in startled surprise when Hayden said, "Jackson, I wish you and Jim Stevenson would take an ambulance and go down into Colorado to do some photography in the Pike's Peak area."

"I really should be getting back to Omaha," Jackson protested. "Mollie—"

"Jackson," Hayden said, "I consider your work indispensable to the Survey. I'd like to have you come on the staff as a permanent and salaried member."

"Nothing could please me more," Jackson told him, "but I'll have to talk to Mollie."

"Write to her," Hayden advised. "Tell her that eventually you would be living in Washington, D.C. I think your Mollie would like Washington."

Jackson wrote her before he left Colorado. By the time he reached Denver, he had his answer. "The position with the Survey would put you a step forward in a promising career. Mr. Hayden is right. I think I'd like Washington."

Before Jackson had finished his assignment in the Pike's Peak area he had an urgent letter from Hayden asking him to go to Washington for a month to help print and catalogue pictures for promoting conservation and for justifying continuance of the Survey.

The month in Washington stretched to two. Shortly before Jackson had planned to return to Omaha, Hayden came into his studio with a map in his hands. "I believe that next summer we should explore Coulter's Hell," said Hayden, spreading the map out on a table. "I'd like to know more about the geology of the region."

While he stood looking at the blank space Hayden pointed out on the map, Jackson recalled what he had heard about the area. Because of the unlikely stories told by explorer John Coulter of holes in the ground that smoked or shot up hot water, the region was popularly known as Coulter's Hell or Brimstone Basin.

"I'd like a chance to explore that country with a camera," said Jackson.

Hayden began to pace up and down the room. "If the geysers are there, photographs would give proof no one could contradict."

Up to the moment that he boarded the train that would carry him to Omaha and to Mollie, Jackson was daydreaming about taking portraits of gushers and smokeholes.

During the winter in Omaha Jackson had almost more studio business than he could handle. He was convinced, though, that his decision to cast his lot with the Survey had been a right one. This conviction deepened when Hayden wrote to say that the pictures taken the preceding summer had contributed much to making the Survey widely and favorably known.

In May 1871 Jackson had word that the Summer Survey team would assemble on June 1 near Ogden in Utah Territory. Mollie would again manage the studio. Jackson insisted that she should first have a vacation and suggested that she go as far as Ogden with him.

They left Omaha in a holiday mood. All along the Union Pacific right-of-way he pointed out scenes associated with past ventures—places on the Platte where he and Rock and Crowl had dickered with Indians or camped for the night;

places in Utah where Hull and he, two summers ago, had set up their outdoor studio.

In eastern Utah the train proceeded cautiously over a trestle spanning a canyon. Mollie turned momentarily away from the view toward Jackson. "Your photographs will give this beauty to all America, to all the world!" she said.

Jackson squeezed Mollie's hand appreciatively, and then sat staring at the red- and orange-tinted rocks. Somehow he must make Mollie's predictions come true. The spirit and majesty of this land unmarred by man-made ugliness *ought* to be given to all America, to all the world.

Members of a Survey party, photographed by Jackson

10: *Brimstone Basin*

JACKSON reluctantly put Mollie on the train that would carry her from Ogden to Omaha. Their trip together had been like a second honeymoon, he thought as he turned away and headed for Survey headquarters. At the camp on the bank of a stream Hayden, looking energetic and purposeful, came striding toward him. "Good to see you, Jack," he said, shaking hands vigorously.

After a rapid exchange of questions and answers, Hadyen turned toward a group of young men in flannel shirts and heavy boots and called, "Dixon, come here a minute, will you?" Then in an aside to Jackson he said, "Young medical student. I'm assigning him to you as an assistant."

"I'm keen about cameras," said Dixon. "Could I see the equipment you'll be using?"

"I have three types," said Jackson taking the cameras out of

their protective boxes. "An eight by ten, a six and a half by eight, and a stereo. All wet-plate process."

Dixon was fascinated by the drop shutter actuated by a rubber band which Jackson had rigged up to cut exposure time from the usual five seconds to a tenth of a second. The lesson in photography was interrupted when colleagues of the summer before began to whoop their greetings as they approached the camp.

On June 10, the Survey team, numbering thirty-five men, broke camp. As they traveled across the Divide, down the Portugal River, and then down the Snake, Jackson discovered that he and the artist Thomas Moran shared many of the same ideals about accuracy and honesty in life and in art. A frail-looking man, who wore his sombrero at a jaunty angle, Moran was friendly and outgoing. Having become interested in photography, he asked innumerable questions. In return he often gave hints that helped Jackson make more artistic pictures.

It took four weeks for the Survey party to reach Fort Ellis

on the East Gallatin River. There, because of hostile Indians
in the area, the commanding officer sent with them a small detachment of soldiers headed by Lieutenant Doane. Thirty miles
beyond the fort, at a ranch owned by a genial trio of brothers,
Jackson was surprised to see J. Crissman, the photographer
who had let him use his studio when he and Hull had been in
Utah Territory.

"I'm located at Bozeman in Montana Territory now,"
Crissman explained. "Hayden invited me to join the expedition here."

Before leaving the ranch, the Survey party transferred their
gear from wagons to pack mules. As the expedition pushed
along a narrow trail, Jackson saw smoke signals rising at
several places along the walls of the canyon.

"Indians reporting on every move we make," said Lieutenant
Doane, riding up beside him. "We'll be safe if we can reach
Yellowstone ahead of them. They fear the region's mysterious
fumes and vapors."

That afternoon the Survey group arrived at Mammoth
Springs, where water flowed over the steplike terraces of a
two hundred foot hill. Jackson stood marveling at the scallops
and beads of scarlet, green, and yellow formed by minerals
that had precipitated from the water.

"Shall I get the camera ready?" asked Dixon, rushing up to
him.

"By all means," Jackson responded. He set up his darkroom
in the shade of an ancient cedar. "I only wish we could
photograph this in its true colors," Dixon said as Jackson
began mixing solutions.

Under ordinary circumstances it took about forty-five minutes to carry out all the processes required for one picture. But having hot spring water at hand for developing cut the drying time so that the photographic team averaged about fifteen minutes to a picture.

Jackson had expected to see geysers as soon as the expedition left Mammoth Springs, but instead he found rushing rivers and canyons. To get pictures of Tower Falls flanked by steep walls of basaltic columns, he had to maneuver his camera to the bottom of the gorge. Dixon delivered plates wrapped in a wet cloth.

After the exposure, Jackson left the camera there and clambered laboriously up the steep wall to develop the plate. Five round trips exhausted him, but the results repaid his efforts.

The Grand Canyon of the Yellowstone River was even more spectacular with the green glint of falls frothing into white. For a week, while the geologists surveyed and collected specimens, Jackson, Crissman, and Dixon photographed. Usually Moran and Elliot, an artist who had been with the Survey the previous summer, painted at easels nearby, shouting back and forth to make themselves heard above the noise of the water.

Leaving the falls, the party passed through stands of fir and spruce where flowers of every season bloomed all at once —larkspur, gentians, Indian paintbrush. In the woods lived deer, porcupine, and bears.

He was in the midst of some of the grandest scenery in the world, Jackson congratulated himself daily, and he and Crissman were the first photographers to have a chance at capturing it with cameras. He joined in the jests and jibes about long hours of work and lack of comforts, but beneath the levity lay a loyalty to the Survey which he knew the others shared.

One night when the men had gathered around a campfire the conversation turned to the future of the land they had been exploring. "It's a great country for hunting and fishing," said a young assistant who had jumped up to add wood to the fire. "Some day smart businessmen will fence it in, turn it into a pleasure ground, and make a million dollars."

Hayden, who had been resting against a saddle, sat up and leaned forward, saying sharply, "If the nation doesn't act quickly, fortune hunters will do just that."

"What's your idea for use of the land?" asked Potato John.

"Making it available to everyone instead of a few," Hayden replied. "I expect to agitate for a national park."

And when the time comes I'll provide the photographs, thought Jackson.

Several days later, on a solo expedition west of Yellowstone Lake, he stumbled on a whole basin of geyser cones and caught one in the process of eruption.

"Can't we move our tents to that area?" he asked Hayden as soon as he returned to camp.

"Time is running out," Hayden told him. "And so are our supplies. The geologists have completed mapping the shoreline and sounding depths in Yellowstone Lake, and I think we'll have to start back."

Jackson tried to stifle his disappointment. After all, he had four hundred pictures without adding any more geyser ones.

But he couldn't free himself from the feeling he'd missed an opportunity that might not come again. He was even more dejected when Lieutenant Doane, who had headed the detachment of soldiers shared by the Hayden party and a group of engineers, also in Yellowstone that summer, said, "The other outfit had a camera toter too—T. J. Hines."

For a moment Jackson felt defeated and defrauded because he would not be the first to provide Yellowstone pictures to stereo viewers. Hines had a national reputation and his photographs were bound to be excellent. But then his sense of sportsmanship came to the fore. The important thing was that people would become aware of the possibilities and necessity for a national park.

The Survey returned to the ranch where they had left their wagons and moved with all possible speed to Fort Hall in Idaho Territory, then in a southeasterly direction to Evanston, on the Union Pacific, where the party disbanded.

"You've given me a lot, both in the field of photography and philosophy," Moran told Jackson. "Even if we should never meet again, I'll count you as a lifelong friend."

"I can say the same," Jackson replied, for Moran had been an ideal companion.

That autumn, at Hayden's request, Jackson revisited Omaha and Pawnee villages, adding to his stock of negatives from 1868. He was much impressed by Dr. Painter, who had left a thriving medical practice in Baltimore to become agent at the Omaha Reservation. He seemed unusually talented and understanding.

After Jackson returned to Omaha, he and Mollie went

ahead with plans for moving to Washington. When Jackson
had to sell the studio at a sacrifice he wondered if he had made
the right decision. Soon there would be a third member in the
family. Would his government salary be adequate? An un-
expected good income from sales of the Yellowstone pictures
eased his anxiety. Because all of Hines' photographs were
destroyed in the disastrous Chicago fire October 8, 1871,
Jackson's pictures were, after all, the first ones seen by stereo
viewers across the nation. Sympathy for his fellow photographer's misfortune deprived him of some of the joy he would
otherwise have experienced.

On their way to Washington, where they would make their
home, Bill and Mollie visited his parents, who had moved to
Nyack, New York, on the Hudson. Bill was thoroughly enjoying the role of a son once more when a letter came from Hayden.
"The bill to establish Yellowstone as a national park will be
considered soon," he had written. "I need prints. I need you."

Bill's parents, who had become very fond of Mollie, begged
her to stay with them until after the baby was born. Jackson
very much wanted her with him, but he decided that it would
be selfish to subject her to house hunting and living among
strangers when she could be so lovingly cared for in his
parents' home.

On the train headed for Washington, he tried to concentrate
on how he could use his pictures to help Hayden state con-
vincingly his plan for an unspoiled wonderland. Over and over
in Jackson's mind drummed the words—a park for all the
people.

Working in
the Grand Tetons,
1872

11: *Grief and Grandeur*

IN WASHINGTON Jackson became involved in the plans of
the group working to have Yellowstone declared a national
park. This he enjoyed, but his leisure hours stretched out
long and empty without Mollie. Hayden had married recently,
and Jackson did not want to intrude on his home life. He

felt less lonely when his brother Fred came to work with him.

In December the Honorable William Claggett of Montana introduced a bill in the House of Representatives proposing that the Yellowstone area be withdrawn from sale or settlement. Newspapers and persons who had seen Jackson's pictures of Yellowstone exerted pressure for passage of the bill. "Jackson's photographs of Yellowstone prove that the truth about the area is more remarkable than the exaggerations we've heard about it," wrote one editor.

But Hayden and others working in behalf of the legislation became discouraged when congressmen remained indifferent or lukewarm. One day, when Hayden dropped in at Jackson's photographic studio in the Department of the Interior, he stood for a moment lost in moodiness; then his face brightened. "Jack, what would you think of circulating some of your Yellowstone scenes in the Senate just before the bill comes up for a vote?" he said.

"I can't see passing them around one by one," said Jackson. "Of course, if you had them in folio form—"

"That's it!" exclaimed Hayden, snapping his fingers. "A booklet to place on the desk of each senator."

"Do you realize how much individual folios would cost?" asked Jackson.

"They'd be worth it," said Hayden, his eyes aglow with enthusiasm.

The folios, completed early in 1872, included pictures of Mammoth Hot Springs, Tower Falls, and other scenic highlights. Each handsomely bound booklet bore on its cover the name of a senator stamped in gold.

Jackson could hardly wait to hear the outcome of the measure. "What a shame it would be," he told Fred, "to have the geysers and forests fall into the hands of greedy money grabbers."

Before the fate of the bill had been decided, Jackson had word from his mother that Mollie was seriously ill. He left for Nyack immediately

Mollie died in childbirth. The baby, a girl, lived only a few hours.

Stunned and heartsick, Jackson returned to Washington. During the days he had spent in Nyack, the park bill, which everyone had expected would be bitterly debated in the Senate, had passed without a dissenting vote.

"Mollie would have been pleased to know that your photographs were a link in the chain of events leading to the establishment of America's first national park," Fred said to comfort him.

Successes meant little to Jackson without Mollie to share them. Although he managed to do what was required of him, a shadow hovered over him. It would be easier, he thought, when he could be outdoors again with the Survey team.

Weeks before the team was to leave for the 1872 trip, Hayden assigned Jackson to a small outfit, headed by James Stevenson, to explore the Three Tetons south of Yellowstone. Later this group would join Hayden in Yellowstone.

Jackson was sure that to do justice to the Tetons he would need to make larger prints than before. Photographs could not then be enlarged, so this meant that he must use a larger camera. But a big camera would mean bigger glass plates, which would be heavy to carry. And how could he get them coated with collodion if he continued to work with the old darkroom box? He finally decided on an 11-by-14-inch camera and provided himself with a tent to serve as a darkroom.

The Teton area impressed Jackson even more than Yellowstone, on the day he and the Stevenson party rode toward the gaunt peaks where icy streams foamed and roared. As a site for their base camp, they chose Pierre's Hole, named for an old French traveler. Chipmunks scolded while Jackson and his assistant, P. V. Beveridge, pitched a tent over the grassy floor dappled by monkshood, gentians, and wild geraniums.

While Stevenson and his aides began mapping the area, Jackson demonstrated the use of equipment to his youthful photographic team and outlined procedures for a side trip away from the base camp.

"I notice your tent is lined with orange calico," said John Merle Coulter, a recent graduate of Hanover College. "Is that to cut out the sun's actinic rays?"

"Exactly," Jackson replied with an approving glance at the young botanist. Intelligent and already dedicated to the work of the Survey, Coulter gave promise of becoming a capable assistant.

"What's our objective?" asked Jackson's brother-in-law, Charley Campbell. Although Charley was only eighteen, Jackson had included him in the party because he thought it would have pleased Mollie.

"Our objective," Jackson said, "will be to reach the main plateau of the Tetons, presumably at an altitude of about eleven thousand feet. From there I hope to be able to get close enough to the Grand Teton to make a face-to-face shot."

When the photographic party set off, it included Beveridge, Coulter, Charley, and a packer named Aleck. For a week Jackson and his aides climbed up steep slopes, across snow-fields, over piles of rocky debris, searching for a vantage point from which to photograph the Grand Teton. But every day they were blocked by barriers of rock and ice, and they returned to their tents discouraged and exhausted.

"It's today or never," said Jackson as they sat eating their breakfast on the eighth morning. "We're due back at the base camp."

Without too much difficulty they climbed up past lodgepole pines, Engelmann's spruce, and alpine firs, which grow up to the timberline. Finally the party reached a high plateau, but as had happened on previous trails, a wall of rock cut off their view of the Grand Teton.

"See that ledge," Charley Campbell said thoughtfully. "Couldn't we—"

"It's narrow and winding," Aleck objected. "And the snow would make it very slippery."

Jackson stood debating with himself. He wanted pictures of the Grand Teton more than he had wanted anything for a long time, but did he have a right to expose his assistants to the dangers of the ledge? One false move could mean death in the gorge below.

"Let's try it," Coulter said eagerly.

The assistants registered their approval by picking up the items for which each one was responsible. Jackson led off.

Before each new step he probed the snow with his boot. Once, when his foot skidded off into space, he had a sickening sensation of dizziness, but a moment's pause restored control.

After what seemed hours the party emerged on the brink of the icy gorge of Glacier Creek, which lay thousands of feet below. Directly in front of them towered the snow-coated Grand Teton, shimmering in the sun.

Jackson had the exalted feeling that comes with achieving a hard-won goal.

"From here, the world looks great, wide, and beautiful," Beveridge said in a hushed tone. Then he turned away and busied himself setting up the darkroom tent and unpacking supplies.

Jackson was preparing his camera when he remembered that he would need water for the developing process. Around him lay only rocks, snow, and ice. "Any of you have anything left in your water bags?" he asked. "I should have planned for extra water, but we've always found streams before."

"Look," said Aleck, "trickling from under the ice over there."

Gleefully the assistants dashed off to fill their water bags while Jackson retreated to his tent to prepare a plate. As he was working he heard a sound of movement outside and cautiously lifted the flap of the tent. On a ledge not twenty feet way stood a mountain sheep! Without moving a muscle, Jackson stared at the animal's massive curly horns. The sheep stared back. If only he could get a picture, thought Jackson. Just then the sheep, startled by the voices of the young men returning with water, disappeared in one powerful leap.

Jackson, with the help of his assistants, took picture after picture of the Grand Teton from different angles and in varied light. Only after he had used up his entire supply of plates did he give the signal to pack. On the way down the mountain he had the feeling that his life would never be the same again. He knew now why some men *had* to climb mountains. In high places they could for a time shed the tension and confusion of daily living.

Two days later Jackson and his assistants rejoined the Stevenson party, and in mid-August they united forces with Hayden in the Lower Fire Hole Basin. The expedition now numbered sixty men.

As they traveled northward along the Fire Hole River, the hollow drumming of horses' hoofs upon the white crust indicated caverns below. Trees bordering the area were either scorched or dead.

One day at their camp on the Fire Hole River, Jackson heard a tremendous rumbling. The earth quivered. Then near the edge of the river a column of water gushed up perhaps two hundred feet. The steam ascended even higher.

"If only my camera had been ready," Jackson said dolefully.

"There'll be plenty of other chances," the park superintendent said.

The next day, after Hayden had assigned each scientist of the party a specific geyser to study, Jackson went off alone. Built up around the geyser basins he found cones of mineral deposits ranging in shape from beehives to castles, and he saw pools of water so clear that they reflected the clouds in the sky. But the only active geysers he discovered erupted feebly, lifting water only a few feet into the air. Jackson was about to turn back to camp when Coulter called excitedly, "Come here a minute, will you?"

Jackson turned around just in time to see a spectacular tower of water and steam rising. "I never seem to have my camera set up at the right time any more," he said to Coulter when the impressive and tremendous outburst had ended.

"Get ready for about an hour from now," Coulter suggested. "I've been watching this geyser all morning, and it erupts almost on a fixed schedule."

At the next performance of the geyser, Jackson took a picture that turned out very well. Hayden, after he had examined the photograph and heard Coulter's account of his observations, exclaimed, "This must be the geyser earlier explorers called Old Faithful!"

During the days that followed, both the geysers and the weather provided Jackson with ideal conditions for photography.

After his return to Washington, his pictures received wide publicity and circulation. "Vivid detail . . . panoramic scope . . . excellent techniques . . ." were some of the phrases newspapers and magazines used in praising his work.

During the day Jackson lost himself in classifying and cataloguing pictures and providing endless copies of them for magazines. But in the evening he was possessed by a restless loneliness. Hungry for companionship with someone who shared his interest in Indians and photography, he wrote long letters to Dr. Painter, agent at the Omaha Reservation. As the months passed, most of the replies were written by Dr. Painter's daughter Emilie, who expressed great interest in Jackson's work and welfare. Her unselfishness and gentleness reminded him of Mollie.

That winter Hayden announced that the Survey trip for 1873 would start from Denver. Jackson immediately made plans to go by way of Nebraska and visit his brother Ed and the Painter family. In Blair he and Ed spent two days reminiscing about their boyhood, the Civil War, and their experiences in Omaha.

When Jackson arrived at the agency on May 4, it seemed to him that Emilie was even more gifted and charming than he remembered her. Encouraged by her sympathetic response, he found himself telling her of his dream to find and photograph a mountain in Colorado which supposedly had a massive cross of snow. "Explorers and Indians insist that there is such a mountain, but they never say exactly where it is," he explained.

"You will find it," Emilie said confidently. "And I hope you will bring me pictures of it."

Jackson longed to have this talented, lovely woman as his wife. But would she have him? Did he have a right to ask any woman to stay at home alone while he went off every summer with Survey parties?

Shortly before he had to leave for Denver on May 12, Jackson screwed up his courage to ask Emilie to marry him. "I don't know what we could do about the summers," he said. "Photography is my business, but—"

"I won't *like* having you away from home," Emilie said, gesturing with her expressive hands. "But I will want you to do what your work demands."

"Then you *will* marry me?" said Jackson, feeling as if he had come up out of darkness into the light of day.

"As soon as your summer Survey trip is over," Emilie promised.

That he had a partner who would understand his dreams gave Jackson a renewed sense of purpose as he rode toward Colorado. When the train neared Denver, he could see the long spine of the vast, uncharted Rockies. Photographing them would require even more patience, courage, and hard work than the Grand Tetons. But he felt equal to any challenge that their snow-capped peaks might offer.

12: *Quest for a Cross of Snow*

J<small>ACKSON</small> looked forward to a reunion with friends as he rode toward Survey headquarters several miles west of Denver. The camp was set up in neat rows of tents at the juncture of Clear Creek and the South Platte River.

As soon as Jackson alighted from the train, John Merle Coulter, the young botanist who had been with him in the Tetons, rushed up, asking, "How are you and your Magic Eye?"

"Great!" Jackson replied. "Last time I saw you, you were hoping to polish off your master's degree. Did you?"

Coulter nodded. Then he introduced a slender, reliable-looking youth who was with him. "This is Jim Cole—son of Senator Cole."

"What's your specialty?" asked Jackson.

"Birds, sir," said Jim, "but I'll help in any way I can."

Hayden, delayed in the East, had delegated supervision of the camp to the expedition's chief topographer, James T. Gardiner.

"Do you think you could take a photographic team and

leave ahead of the other two Survey divisions?" the heavy-set, black-bearded man asked.

"The sooner the better," Jackson replied.

"This will be your intinerary." Gardiner unrolled a large map on the rough camp table. His forefinger traced a trail marked on the map with India ink. "On July tenth," he said, "you'll meet Hayden in Fairplay, Colorado."

"And then?" asked Jackson.

Gardiner shrugged. "Hayden said something about going into the area around the headwaters of the Arkansas and trying to find that mountain trappers claim has a cross of snow on it."

If it's in Colorado, I'll find it, Jackson vowed silently to himself. To take a picture of it for Emilie would be the biggest goal of the summer.

Jackson felt like a general in command of an army as he rode off with his assistants on horseback the morning of May 24. He realized that heading his own crew would bring greater responsibilities. Before this he had had to think only of chemicals and cameras. Now he must keep his men fed, sheltered, healthy, and satisfied.

Besides Coulter and Cole, the team included Potato John, two veteran packers, Bill Whan and Tom Cooper, and Lieutenant W. L. Carpenter. On leave from the Army, Carpenter would act as entomologist for the Survey.

It took five days for them to reach the Long's Peak region. There Jackson took pictures of the peak and other scenic mountains. Then he shepherded his assistants southward through sparsely inhabited country along trails worn by deer, Indians, trappers, and prospectors. In forests the men sometimes had to hack their way through underbrush. Several times mules bogged down in snowdrifts left by winter storms. Almost every afternoon a brief but brisk mountain shower drenched the explorers.

Most of the time skies were clear. To overcome the unusual brightness of the high, thin air, Jackson had to use smaller apertures and longer exposures than usual. He had to remember that in the crystal-clear air peaks that might be miles away appeared to be within easy walking distance.

Whenever the team came to a peak, and they came to them often, Jackson established a base camp. While he photographed the peak, other members of the party surveyed, observed, collected rocks and plants. Cole listened to trills of warblers and the metallic calls of Rocky Mountain jays.

Jackson knew that in the future probably hundreds of photographers would take pictures of the gorges and peaks of the West, but at the moment he and his camera were pioneers. This knowledge kept him going on slopes so steep that he had trouble packing heavy equipment to a vantage point. His photographs, when fitted together with the topographical and scientific information contributed by the other members of the Survey, would provide exact information on the appearance, resources, and wildlife of the region.

Jackson and his assistants worked from sunup to sundown, and at night they lolled around a big crackling campfire. Their singing and laughter made a brave racket in the wilderness. Sometimes Jackson amused himself by picturing Potato John and the packers in the situations of the songs they sang so lustily—"dwelling in marble halls" or "dying for Annie Laurie."

Outside Central City, a bustling mountain town, the party camped for several days. Quartermaster James Stevenson, a friend of Jackson's during the Yellowstone survey, rode up from Denver to bring mail and supplies. Jackson read and re-read every word Emilie had written. There was no question about her loyalty and understanding, he thought happily.

After several days of photographing scenery in this vicinity, the team moved to Southwest. Because Bill Whan was needed in Denver to help with the maintenance of Survey parties, he had been replaced by another experienced packer, Harry Bishop.

At the outskirts of Georgetown, Jackson fell behind the party to take a picture. When he rode into town on horseback he found Harry Bishop and Tom Cooper surrounded by a group of loudly complaining citizens.

"What's going on?" asked Jackson.

"We were coming down the street peaceful like—" Harry started to explain.

". . . when the goldanged mules bolted." Tom finished.

"One of them busted my fence," exploded a belligerent red-haired man. "And I want damages."

"We'll repay you for any loss," Jackson said soothingly. "We're with the Hayden Survey and—"

Before he could finish the sentence, the red-haired man exclaimed, "The Survey! You must be that picture-takin' Jackson. Forget about the fence. I reckon your photographs will give this country plenty of free advertisin'!"

When he left Georgetown, Jackson continued his leg-weary-ing ascents of peaks—Grays, Torreys, McClelland, and others. In South Park, travel became easier because of ranches and roads, but the summer sun had turned scorching hot and mosquitoes plagued the party.

On July 1 the team reached the Garden of the Gods, where wind and water had eroded red sandstone rocks into weird, fantastic formations. A cameraman's paradise, thought Jackson, as he photographed a formation that looked like two camels kissing!

To Emilie he wrote that he would have to put aside cameras for a few days and press toward Fairplay, where he would meet Hayden. Expressing his eagerness to hurry back to the "sweetest girl in the world," he closed with "Your devoted Will."

At the post office in Fairplay a letter from Hayden notified Jackson of a delay. During the enforced vacation, he checked on supplies, and had the mules reshod. Reluctantly he re-placed the travel-worn horse he had been riding with a white mule named Dolly. A holiday atmosphere prevailed at the camp after the outfits led by A. D. Wilson and the brilliant geographer Henry Gannett joined them—all waiting for Hayden.

Unable to stay away from his cameras very long, Jackson photographed Mt. Lincoln and the Montezuma silver mine. When one of the miners volunteered the information that he had been in Arkansas River country, Jackson asked, "Ever see a mountain around there with a snowy cross?"

"Wal no, I've never seen it, but I've heard about it," the miner said.

"Where is it?" asked Jackson.

The miner rubbed his bristly chin reflectively. "You likely could see it from Notch mountain. That's 'cross the Divide."

"I think I've found out the approximate location of the mountain with the snowy cross," Jackson told Hayden when he arrived in Fairplay July 13.

Hayden seemed almost as enthusiastic about reaching it as Jackson was. "When we leave here," he said, "we'll go in separate parties, but travel parallel to each other. We'll unite forces in the vicinity of Notch mountain and look for the snowy cross."

In the high, rugged mountains west of Fairplay, Dolly proved to be sturdy and untiring. But breakdown of equipment, miry roads, rock-and-log-scattered canyons tested tempers. As leader of the group, Jackson had to stay on an even keel, but he found it hard to remain cheerful when the sun's glare or wind-driven dust ruined otherwise good pictures.

He became even more discouraged the day fitful snow flurries forced him to abandon the ascent of La Plata Peak. Hurrying down the mountainside with Coulter and Bishop, he slipped on a wet rock, wrenched his ankle, and broke the tray he used for the solution in which he bathed his pictures.

On August 10, Hayden showed up with his team. That morning Jackson climbed to a high divide between the East River and Rock Creek. He had been working only a short time when Potato John came panting up the slope. "Gimlet came a cropper," he said breathlessly. "And his pack slipped. Your glass pictures are a-layin' around in splinters."

Sick with dismay, Jackson hurried toward the scene of the accident. As he neared the place where Gimlet had stumbled he saw Dr. Hayden staring glumly at a heap of shattered glass. "Who's responsible for this mess?" he asked irritably.

"No one person, I'm sure," said Jackson. Then he added in an agonized voice, "Every picture I've taken since we left Fairplay is in that heap of broken plates."

"May not be as bad as it looks," said Hayden, suddenly reasonable and sympathetic. "You may be able to salvage some of them."

Jackson found some of the plates intact, others nicked. "Ten of the best ones are smashed," he said tonelessly.

Hayden stood silent for a moment; then he said, "Jack, I know you want to be the first to give this grandeur to the public. I guess you'd better retrace your steps and take the peaks over again."

"I won't let this wreck your timetable," said Jackson, grateful for a second chance.

Replacing his photographs meant days of feverish activity and repetition of strenuous climbs. To make matters worse, food supplies did not come through as expected. But slightly over a week later, Jackson, although close to exhaustion, had pictures of a country on which few men had ever set foot, and which none but he had photographed.

As the Hayden Survey team descended from Tennessee Pass to the headwaters of the Eagle River in the vicinity of Notch mountain, Jackson threw off the effects of overwork and end-of-season weariness. The climax of the summer would be photographing the snowy cross.

For the attempt to locate it, Hayden divided the men into two parties. After breakfast on August 23, Jackson, laden with chemicals and his darkroom tent, struck off for Notch mountain followed by Tom Cooper with the camera and Coulter carrying glass plates. Hayden had already left with a larger team, including staff artist Dr. William H. Holmes, to climb Roche mountain, where the cross supposedly lay.

Tangled masses of underbrush and fallen tree slowed climbing. Every little shrub, wet from the rain of the night before, dumped chilling water. The hip-deep, icy water of a mountain brook left Jackson's teeth chattering. Was there really a snowy cross? he kept asking himself. Eagerness carried him so far ahead of Tom and Coulter that he had to pause occasionally to make sure they were coming.

At the summit, Jackson found naked, jagged, slate-colored rocks with a few patches of snow here and there. Immediately he looked off in the direction of Roche mountain, hoping to see the cross, but thick cottony clouds completely hid the peak.

Thinking that the clouds might part, Jackson sat down to watch. When the raw, biting wind chilled him to the bone, he wrapped the darkroom tent around him. Two hours passed. Why hadn't Coulter and Tom caught up? A terrifying sense of isolation and anxiety gripped Jackson. He started to make a descent, but then decided it would be best to stay where he was.

Finally he heard Coulter shouting, "Hallo, Jack, Hallo!"

"This way," called Jackson.

"We're stuck!" yelled Tom.

Jackson groped his way down through the fog toward their voices. As he led the way back to the summit, he saw in the valley below them a rainbow forming a complete circle. He hoped it was a promise of better conditions for photography, but when they reached the crest clouds still hid Roche mountain.

With the approach of sunset the air turned much colder. "We can't stay here all night, Jack," Coulter protested.

"Suppose we drop back to timberline where we can find wood for a fire," Jackson suggested. "We can try again tomorrow."

The trio cached the photographic equipment under some overhanging rocks, then wearily retreated to the timberline. In the gun-metal gloom of descending twilight, they collected a huge pile of wood. As the night wore on Jackson dozed occasionally but then roused himself to add fuel to the fire.

Before sunup the trio, although shivering and hungry, again began the ascent. Jackson's knees were wobbly from his lack of food and he had never been thirstier, but he kept on climbing. At the summit a few clouds still hovered over Roche mountain but gave promise of lifting soon.

"Little pool of water in the rocks over here," shouted Tom. There was a tinkle as he cracked the thin crust of ice on the surface. Jackson's tiredness drained away as he lapped up a cold drink. Now wide awake he turned toward Roche mountain. On its rocky breast lay a snowy cross sparkling like diamonds. For a moment Jackson stood with the others in silent wonder. Then, his heart pounding with excitement, he went to get his darkroom tent.

"You've done it!" Coulter exclaimed later, looking at the clearly defined cross. "You've photographed a mountain most people didn't believe existed."

"The snowy cross will make you famous," added Tom.

Fame would be empty, thought Jackson, compared to the satisfaction he felt at this moment. The photographs, probably the best he had ever taken, were worth all that they had cost in time, aching muscles, and discouragement, if only those who viewed them could feel the grandeur of the dazzling, sun-smitten cross.

13: *Uncooperative Utes and Lost Cities*

A<small>T THE</small> end of the summer of photographing peaks and what is now known as the Mount of the Holy Cross, Jackson revisited the Omaha reservation. He and Emilie were married October 8, 1873. After a honeymoon in New York City, they rented rooms in Washington at a comfortable boarding house close to Survey headquarters.

They lived quietly, occasionally going to dinner with friends or attending a lecture. But they really preferred to stay at home to talk, read, or play cribbage or chess. On Sundays they often took the train to Baltimore where Emilie had friends and relatives. Jackson noticed that strangers frequently turned to admire Emilie, very stylish in a dress with a long ruffled skirt and a bustle.

Jackson's photographs of the Rocky Mountains, many of which were sold to magazines, built up his reputation. Income from these sales tided him over for several months that winter when Congress, hard-pressed to meet urgent governmental needs, postponed payment of Survey salaries.

Jackson would have reopened a studio but Hayden, confident that funds would be forthcoming, persuaded him to wait. "The Survey and the West need a recording artist," Hayden told him. "I don't know of a single photographer whose work matches yours."

Jackson had no such estimate of himself, but he felt the Survey had helped him to achieve his true purpose in life and loyally agreed to stand by.

Not until early in July did Congress finally make funds available for a summer Survey. Delay in appropriations meant that Hayden had to organize the expedition hastily. As he and Jackson discussed final plans at the camp outside Denver, Hayden glanced at two teen-age boys lolling on the grass. "I'm dubious," he said, "about your aides Ed Anthony and Frank Smart—they've had no experience roughing it." Hayden's fingers drummed nervously on the table. "You may not eat so well either. I've had to replace Potato John with a cook named Charlie."

"At least there's one known quantity," said Jackson, "and that's Dolly." He had been pleased to find his faithful mule of the previous summer among the Survey animals.

When Jackson left the camp on July 21, his party included Charlie the cook, the two teen-age Easterners, packers Mitchell and Stevens, and Ernest Ingersoll, who, although young, had already made a reputation as a correspondent. He would serve as a naturalist on the Survey.

Jackson's objective was Los Pinos, the Ute Indian reservation in the southwest corner of Colorado. Bad weather, rugged trails, and uncooperative mules delayed the photographic team. Ingersoll did more than his share of camp chores and cheered Jackson when discouragement threatened. But Anthony and Smart often irritated Jackson and other members of the party because of their pranks and their indifference toward the work of the Survey.

At Los Pinos reservation—a cluster of dwellings, a mill, blacksmith shop, and schoolhouse—agent Henry Bond and his wife welcomed the party with obvious pleasure. Bond promised cooperation in helping Jackson photograph the Utes but warned that they were superstitious about cameras. He also suggested a camp site on a stream about three quarters of a mile from the Agency buildings.

"Make things shipshape," Jackson directed Anthony and Smart. "We'll be spending some time in this area."

Next day Bond told Jackson, "Chief Ouray is our best hope for your project. He speaks English, is a promoter of peace, and is, on the whole, friendly toward whites and their way of life."

Ouray lived in a little house, built for him in return for service to the government. The dignified chief, who had two braids of long black hair, greeted Jackson and Bond in English. Then with a sweep of the hand he motioned them to stools. The Indian blankets, pottery, and urn-shaped baskets, decorated in red and black, contrasted strangely with Ouray's dark broadcloth suit and shiny boots. Jackson was delighted with the intelligent, alert questions Ouray put to him about the Survey.

When the conversation shifted to photography, the chief readily consented to pose with his wife Chipeta. Shortly after

Jackson had converted the Agency porch to a studio, Ouray arrived wearing a buckskin costume laden with fringe, beads, and medals that glinted in the sun. Chipeta, a very attractive woman, had a white deerskin dress with thick white fringe, elaborate beadwork, and porcupine-quill embroidery.

After Jackson had photographed Chief Ouray and his wife, the agent took him to an encampment of Utes. It was only a temporary camp, which had been set up to accommodate Indians who on the following day would claim the annual supplies furnished by the government.

The first Utes to whom Bond talked flatly refused to have their pictures taken. But Peah, a youthful chief who had dramatic mannerisms, offered to cooperate. Jackson had made only a few photographs when raindrops began to splash on his equipment. Peah invited Jackson and Bond into his tepee, where he entertained them, speaking alternately in English, Spanish, Ute, and sign language. When conversation lagged, an unidentified elderly man in the corner of the tepee exclaimed happily, "Heap lazy." By the time the rain ended, it was too late for further photography.

Both Jackson and Bond hoped that when the Indians assembled the next day to claim their rations they would be too intent on beans, flour, sugar, and tobacco to notice photographic preparations. Early that morning, Jackson set up his camera outdoors and then went to the Bonds' kitchen to process a plate. When he came back, he found a group of Indians surrounding the camera. "Will you stand back, please, so I can take a picture?" he asked, as courteously as possible.

No one budged. Jackson inserted the plate in his camera

and then attempted to focus. No sooner had he crouched under the focusing cloth than a Ute in loin cloth and moccasins snatched it off. A companion tossed a blanket over the lens.

Jackson straightened up and stood silent for a moment, wondering what to do. On the weather-beaten bronzed faces he detected distrust and hostility. With relief he saw Peah striding toward him. But the chief's face mirrored none of the friendliness of the day before. "No *bueno*," he said harshly. "No *bueno*, to take pictures."

"I don't understand," said Jackson. "You let me photograph you yesterday."

"Cameras do not make a brave warrior lose strength and soul," said Peah. "But maybe make squaw or papoose die. Maybe all die. No *bueno*."

"It's no use," said Bond, as a Ute kicked viciously at the legs of the tripod supporting the camera. "Better come inside."

That night at camp Jackson kept thinking of the motto Hayden had always stressed on Survey trips—"To strive, to seek, to find, and not to yield." Was there some way of appealing to the Utes that he had overlooked?

Jackson was startled when an Indian suddenly appeared before him and announced, "Me Billy." With no further preliminaries he said in a menacing voice, "Hunters come to destroy Ute food. Hunters die. Men come to take gold from Ute mines. Men die."

"But we don't intend to steal anything from you," Jackson protested.

"Black box bad medicine," the Ute said harshly. "Be better if you do not go through Ute lands."

"I guess we won't accomplish anything by staying here," Jackson said dispiritedly after Billy left. It distressed him, he wrote Emilie, to have failed in a goal Hayden had set for him, but he couldn't expose his assistants to possible retaliation from the Utes.

From Los Pinos he and his team headed for Baker's Park, where he was scheduled to meet another team later in the summer. By August 27 they had reached the head of the Rio Grande River. After they had set up camp late in the afternoon, Jackson saw a man detach himself from a pack train that was pitching a camp nearby and come toward him.

"Why, it's E. H. Cooper," he said to Ingersoll. "I knew him in Omaha."

Cooper, who was on his way to a mining camp on the headwaters of the La Plata River, readily accepted the invitation to stay over until morning.

That night as they sat around the campfire he asked a number of questions about the Survey. Then he said, "Seems to me you ought to take pictures of the ruins of the lost cities where Indians used to live."

"Lost cities!" said Smart. "Where?"

"On cliffs in Mancos Canyon," Cooper replied. "Especially in the region called Mesa Verde. That's Spanish for *green table*."

When Jackson wanted more details, Cooper sounded vague. "Come with me to La Plata," he suggested. "John Moss can tell you everything."

"Who's John Moss?" asked Ed Anthony.

"A high muck-a-muck from California. Bosses a crew of

miners, but there ain't much he couldn't tell you about Indians."

Miners were often credulous, thought Jackson. Perhaps they only imagined cities perched on cliffs. But if there really were remnants of lost cities, pictures of them would help to make up for the failure with the Ute Indians.

"I just may see you," Jackson said next morning when Cooper left to rejoin the pack train.

As the photographic party traveled through rough country teeming with bears and mountain lions, Jackson had misgivings about his decision. Would Hayden approve? What if he used up supplies and the energies of his men and got no pictures of lost cities?

At a cluster of tents and brush wickiups on the La Plata River, a wiry man with hair hanging to the shoulders of his buckskin suit greeted Jackson and introduced himself as John Moss. After Jackson explained his purpose, Moss, intelligent and apparently well educated, said he had seen ruins of a cliff-dwelling people and consented to serve as Jackson's guide.

The party, augmented by Moss and Cooper, set off on a crisp September morning in an adventurous mood. Beyond the Mancos River the trail became a rock-strewn menace. No trees grew except small, gnarled piñons. As evening approached, Moss struck down into a canyon with steep, crumbly walls of light yellowish sandstone. "Why not camp here?" he said. "Tomorrow we can climb to a ruined city."

As they basked in the warmth of a sagebrush fire, packer Steve asked skeptically, "Where is this ruined city?"

Moss pointed to a rim of canyon perhaps seven hundred feet above the valley. Staring at the ledge, Jackson saw what looked like the broken walls of houses sandwiched between strata of sandstone. "I'm going to climb up to it," he said excitedly.

"Soon be dark," Cooper warned.

"But if I go up now I can work out the best approach to take tomorrow," Jackson insisted.

Ingersoll jumped up and joined him. The climb was stiff, but they had little difficulty until they were within a short distance of the ledge. Then a steep, vertical wall stopped them.

"I see an old dead tree over to our right," said Ingersoll. "If we propped it against the wall, maybe we could find some of the old foot and hand holds that the Indians used."

When they reached the ledge on which stood remnants of dwellings, Jackson was disappointed. Dirt, debris, and a few pieces of broken pottery littered the floors of ancient dwellings. Then it occurred to Jackson that he and Ingersoll stood where braves must once have poured out prayers to the dawn or guarded their kinsmen against secret attack.

Prowling around what was left of two-storied houses constructed from slabs of sandstone, Jackson wondered what had happened to the cliff dwellers who had perched on the ledge like swallows. Had enemies forced them to flee?

"Shouldn't we start down?" asked Ingersoll. "I don't exactly relish the idea of spending the night with a drove of pack rats."

For a moment, overpowered by a strange silence, Jackson stood staring down at the floor of the canyon, where the red glow of their campfire pushed back the shadows of oncoming night. The only sound was that of the wind singing through the deserted village. Somehow, thought Jackson, he had to get his equipment up to this ledge. Through photographs it should be possible to re-create the proud past of a once-thriving people.

14: *Hopis, Paiutes, and Clay Models*

NEXT MORNING, Jackson, with the help of his assistants, hoisted his camera and supplies up to the ledge. From fragments of pots, baskets, and tools, from seeds and bones, Jackson pieced together something of the life of the cliff dwellers. Braves had probably hunted, grown squash, or chipped out arrows while the women and girls tended papooses, ground corn into meal, and made baskets.

During the next few days, Moss led the little expedition over hazardous trails and into desolate gorges, unpopulated except by hummingbirds, chipmunks, coyotes, and skunks. Jackson discovered many signs of vanished civilization, but because the date for his rendezvous with the Survey team at Baker's Park was almost at hand, he had to work under pressure. September skies remained cobalt and cloudless, but alkali dust sometimes interfered with picture taking. Water was so scarce that in some places the men had to dig holes in dry stream beds to find any to drink.

On September 16 Jackson headed back toward Baker's Park. As the two divisions traveled together toward Denver, rain and snow hampered them. Because of the cold weather, and also because of mountain lions and coyotes that filled the air with blood-curdling cries, Jackson kept an all-night fire whenever possible. If the fire faltered because of damp wood, he encouraged it with a few ounces of the collodion he used to coat glass plates.

Hayden and the public too responded with admiration for Jackson's photographs of the "Lost Cities" which were published after his return to Washington.

"The thing that bothers me," Jackson told Emilie, "is the thought of what lies in the Mesa Verde region still undiscovered and unphotographed."

Emilie reached for a piece of needlework. "You'll go again next summer, won't you?" she asked.

"Hayden wants me to." Jackson studied Emilie's face to see if he could tell whether her question had been asked in a spirit of approval or criticism. "But I hate to leave you for so long a time again, and—"

"Remember," Emilie said, looking up from her sewing, "before we were married I said I wouldn't like having you away, but I would want you to do what your work demanded. I meant it then and I mean it now."

Grateful for her understanding, Jackson discussed with Emilie his plans for the trip. These involved a specially designed 20-by-25-inch camera that would do justice to the ruins at Mesa Verde.

On June 6, 1875, after a brief stopover in Denver, Jackson set off for Mesa Verde with cook Bill Shaw, veteran packers Bob Mitchell and Bill Whan, and E. A. Barber, a naturalist who represented *The New York Times*. At La Plata mining camp Jackson added a guide, Harry Lee, who had been recommended by John Moss.

"We may have some Indian trouble," warned Lee. "The Utes suspect that any parties sent out by the government are scheming to take their land."

But Jackson accumulated a number of satisfactory photographs in the Mesa Verde area with no interference. After leaving there, he and his team pushed westward along the San Juan River and then dipped down into Arizona territory.

Because little was known about the Hopi Indians, Hayden had asked Jackson to photograph their villages and customs. Except for tablelands covered with twisted piñons and silvery juniper, the landscape often presented a sober sameness, but Jackson thought he had never seen bluer skies. Studying the networks of tiny tracks on the tawny sand, he would try to figure out whether they belonged to lizards, birds, or desert mice. When the temperature rose well above a hundred even the hummingbirds, rabbits, and insects became part of the stillness that almost rang in Jackson's ears.

In a long shallow cave along the Chinle Wash, the party unearthed a wealth of grinding basins, ax heads, arrow tips, spear points, and pottery still intact.

"I wish we could take enough specimens to show archaeologists what they've been overlooking out here," Jackson said wistfully.

At Lee's suggestion he wrapped a few pottery pieces in spare bedding and packed them on a sure-footed pack mule called Old Mag. About noon on August 12, Jackson saw stone houses that merged with the mesa upon which they had been built. "Hopi village?" he asked expectantly.

Lee nodded. "It's called Tewa." He went on to explain that once long ago the Tewas had come from the Rio Grande to help the Hopis defend themselves against their enemies and had never gone back home.

When the party reached the foot of a steep trail leading up to the little village, an Indian guard blocked their ascent. Lee, speaking in the Tewa language, explained Jackson's hope of being allowed to take pictures in the village. Then he asked, "Are we welcome?"

"Come," said the man, who identified himself as *Capitán* Tom.

On top of the mesa Tom invited Jackson and the others into his pleasantly cool, flat-roofed home, filled with the aroma of stewed fruit and freshly baked bread. From beams of cottonwood overlaid with brush hung bows and arrows, dried herbs, and painted dolls. Seated on sheepskins, Jackson and his team ate succulent ears of roasted corn, Indian bread, and stewed peaches served by Tom's sister Num-pa-ya, Serpent-that-has-no-tooth.

Afterward Jackson took pictures of the poised, graceful Indian maiden. He coaxed a smile from her by complimenting her on the beauty of the turquoise and silver jewelry she wore. Then Jackson strolled through the crooked streets of the little village overrun by scrawny chickens and mongrel dogs. At intervals he halted to take pictures of women grinding corn and making pottery. Emilie, he thought, would enjoy the quiet women, who seemed uniformly polite and generous.

"Now," said Lee, after Jackson had voiced his thanks and his farewells to the friendly Tewas, "if you want to go to the village of Walpi, I think you'll just about be in time for the rain-making Snake Dance."

By the time the photographers had reached the mesa, villagers had already congregated around the plaza. The Antelope chief appeared first, followed by barefooted Indians wearing little besides embroidered kilts, fox tails, and turquoise beads. Carrying rattles in their hands, they marched around the plaza while the Antelope chief sprinkled sacred corn meal on the ground.

The march ended abruptly. A hush fell over dancers and spectators alike. Then the Snake priests, their bodies daubed with red paint and wearing red kilts, entered armed with eagle-feather whips. While the Antelope priests shook their rattles and sang, the Snake priests gestured and leaped wildly. As the music rose to a frenzied pitch, the Snake priests encircled writhing snakes that had been released. Toward the end of the dance each priest seized one or two snakes and darted down the trail.

"The snakes are supposed to carry rain messages to Nature's hiding place," Lee explained to Jackson.

When the last Snake priest had disappeared, the Antelope priests marched gravely around the plaza four times, then went to their ceremonial chamber, the *kiva*. After the dance, the chief invited Jackson and his party to share the gala feast of roasted meats, Indian bread, corn pudding, and other dainties.

The next two weeks, apart from the discovery of more ruins, very little happened that was exciting. But on August 31, as the party headed down through Montezuma Canyon, Jackson had an uneasy feeling when he saw an Indian boy, half concealed behind the rocks, spying on them.

A short time later, a cloud of dust rolled toward the photographic team. When it lifted, Jackson saw eighteen or twenty young Paiute Indians. Swinging rifles overhead, they rode forward shouting, "Hi, Hi, Hi!"

Harry Lee advanced bravely to meet them and explained that these men were friends of their friend John Moss. Jackson could tell by the expressions on their faces that Lee was making very little headway. Maliciously one of the Paiutes raised his quirt and struck a mule. Others did the same to horses and riders. Instantly the animals galloped in a wild stampede down the canyon. Clinging desperately to his horse, Jackson thought it would be a miracle if they reached the bottom of the canyon alive. Even if they were not thrown and trampled, there was little hope of considerate treatment from the howling, screeching savages who pursued.

At the foot of the canyon the bucks reined their horses to a halt near a cluster of wickiups. Spent by their wild flight, the Survey animals calmed down immediately. An old man, gnarled and twisted as a wind-battered piñon tree, stepped out of one of the wickiups.

"Chief Pogonobogwint," Lee said in an aside to Jackson.

"You are welcome," the chief said. Then he turned toward the brash bucks and with a disapproving wave of the hand dismissed them.

After Lee had explained what had happened, Chief Pogonobogwint shook his head. "Young," he said. "Spend night here," he urged.

But Jackson, shaken by his experiences, felt he wanted to put some distance between himself and the impetuous braves. He did, however, accept the corn boiled in the shucks which the chief offered. Eager to leave the Paiutes behind, Jackson wanted to take the first trail they came to that led out of Montezuma Canyon.

"Too narrow," Lee objected, "and it's not one I know." But in the end he yielded.

They had gone only a short distance up the steep trail when Jackson saw Old Mag halt and begin to crumple. He called reassuring words to her, but she tottered and then disappeared over the brink of the canyon.

Jackson scrambled down the canyon wall with all the speed he could summon. Mag had landed on a springy bush and was uninjured, but Jackson had trouble getting her back onto the trail.

"How about them fancy pots she was packin'?" asked Mitchell.

To his amazement, Jackson found all of them unbroken. "The Smithsonian will have an exhibit after all," he said, relieved.

Working their way back toward Colorado, the photographic team encountered unfriendly Utes all along the way. Later Jackson learned that the Gardiner Survey team in the same area had held off Ute attackers for a period of thirty-six hours. All the men had escaped, but they had lost four mules.

"I guess we were lucky," he told Emilie after he returned to Washington.

Jackson had never been happier than he was that winter. Because they expected a child, he and Emilie moved into a small house. They chose the name Clarence Seymour for the sturdy baby born February 2, 1876.

Jackson had hoped that Congress would declare Mesa Verde a park area, but legislators showed slight interest in such a plan. However, he saw a chance for rousing popular interest in the plan when Hayden asked him to make a three-dimensional panorama of the deserted cities of Mesa Verde. This project, he explained, would be part of the Survey exhibit at the forthcoming Philadelphia Centennial, celebrating the signing of the Declaration of Independence.

While he had been in the Mesa Verde area, Jackson had not only taken photographs but had also made sketches and careful measurements. Using these resources, he and his friend

W. H. Holmes, a Survey staff artist, built scale models of clay. A corps of assistants helped cast and tint them.

One day in the spring of 1876, Hayden said, "I don't believe I'll send you into the field this summer, Jack. It seems to me you could best serve the Survey by being on hand at the Centennial to answer questions about your exhibit and to give lectures."

Jackson liked the idea of being closer to home during the summer. Emilie might even spend part of the time with him in Philadelphia. It would also be interesting to see the other exhibits, but the prospect of lecturing worried him. He enjoyed talking about the Lost Cities to friends, but when he got nervous he stammered, and he would surely be nervous speaking to strangers. And what would it be like to spend a whole summer indoors?

15: *Imageless Films and Failures*

JACKSON was jubilant when the model of the Lost Cities attracted almost as much attention at the Centennial Exposition as Dr. Alexander Graham Bell's telephone. On hot sultry days he longed for the snow-cooled breeze of distant peaks and the resinous tang of evergreen needles, but most of the time he enjoyed the questions put to him by visitors. He even liked lecturing.

Always intent on improving his techniques and methods, Jackson spent most of his off-duty hours studying photographic exhibits. When Emilie came to Philadelphia to keep him company, he described to her his plan for inventing a panoramic camera to record the fair. The biggest snag would be getting a moving, sensitized recording surface. It would be impossible to use a glass plate, and roll film was hardly past the laboratory stage. With a combination of cogs and clockwork, Jackson built a camera that rotated at constant speed through an angle of three hundred and sixty degrees. He solved the problem of suitable film by coating ordinary paper with a collodion emulsion on a sub-stratum of thin rubber.

By the end of the summer, Jackson knew as much as any

person alive about the practical aspects of photography. The Centennial Commission awarded him a bronze medal in recognition of his achievements. The Lost Cities exhibit was sent on to the American Museum of Natural History and other museums and did much to arouse scientific interest in the archaeology of the Southwest.

During the winter of 1876–1877 he became acquainted with Dr. Sheldon Jackson, Superintendent of Home Missions of the Presbyterian Church. "This summer I plan to visit all the Hopi pueblos in New Mexico and Arizona," Dr. Jackson told William Henry. "I wish you and your cameras could go along."

Unique Hopi villages had more appeal for Jackson than the terrain of Wyoming—the objective of the 1877 Survey. When he asked permission to go to the Southwest instead of Wyoming, Hayden told him, "I'd like to build up our file of Hopi photographs, but I can't spare manpower to give you a team of assistants."

"If I used the new dry film I could cut down on bulk and weight and get along without assistants or packers," Jackson pointed out.

From a photographic dealer in London he ordered film described in the catalog as "Sensitive negative tissue supplied in bands. Fully guaranteed."

"It must be a relief," said Emilie, as she helped Jackson prepare for his journey, "to leave all your messy chemicals at home."

"And I won't have to develop each picture as soon as I take

it," Jackson gloated. "I can just file the film and print it after I'm back in my own darkroom with good equipment."

Test prints of the first photographs he took in New Mexico turned out so well that he had no misgivings about storing the rest of the film in tight, waterproof cans.

Jackson took hundreds of photographs of Navajos building hogans, silversmithing, trading, and of Hopis working with primitive hoes, carving *kachina* dolls, dancing, and carrying out daily routines. The pictures would, he knew, add much to the information and understanding of Indian life. He could hardly wait to develop them.

But after the films had been processed in his studio at the Department of the Interior, they turned out blank. Jackson used every method he could think of to make the images appear, but no pictures came through. Both enraged and helpless, he stood glaring at the worthless film. This was the most costly setback of his career. The time Gimlet had stumbled and smashed the plates seemed minor compared to this.

"I suppose the film deteriorated," he explained to Hayden. "Probably I should have anticipated this but after the first test . . ." his voice trailed off despairingly.

"You discovered a valuable ruin in Chaco Canyon and objects of interest to archaeologists," Hayden said to comfort him. "Perhaps you can prepare a written report that will take the place of your photographs."

He could never describe in words the concentration of a Hopi carver or the concern of a little girl mothering a cornhusk doll, Jackson thought miserably.

"Didn't any of the negatives develop out?" Emilie asked in

a shocked tone when Jackson reached home and reported his loss.

"Not a single one," Jackson replied. "I've never had such a complete failure."

The inadequacy of the dry films goaded Jackson into a series of experiments. For the Survey trip to Wyoming in the summer of 1878 he again took dry films, but he also carried the essentials for wet-plate photography.

When Jackson heard that there would be an eclipse of the sun on July 29 he decided to try for a photograph using the wet-plate process. Ten minutes before the predicted contact time, he retreated to his darkroom tent to coat plates. While he spread collodion the interior seemed much gloomier than usual.

"Jack, either our watches are wrong or the eclipse is early," Hayden shouted.

Jackson rushed outside with his wet plate, but by then he could catch only the tail end of the eclipse.

All through August he experimented and recorded results of various cameras, solutions, and developing fluids. Sometimes he used both a wet plate and a dry film for the same scene and compared results. He filled notebooks with comments such as, "First plate (11 x 14) bad. Wavy lines in film. Collodion probably at fault. Next exposure gave collodion longer time to set, kept plates in motion while in the bath. Better than first."

But for Jackson, chemistry, techniques, and timing were only the basic tools. He believed selectivity and sensitivity in response to the changeableness of nature had to enter into really good pictures. Sometimes mules and weather conspired to defeat his attempts. Hoggie, the pack mule, jolted a bath holder in which Jackson had left two plates. The plates were smashed and the plate holder punched full of holes. Haze and wind fogged innumerable plates.

When the Survey party reached Fremont Peak in the Wind River mountains, Jackson was determined to produce a memorable photograph. Steepness of ascent ruled out lugging chemicals for wet-plate photography. Haunted by the imageless negatives of the summer before, he prepared seven plates with Young's bromo-iodide emulsion and dried them over a heated shovel. With these he took photographs that Hayden insisted were the best he had ever made.

From Fremont Peak the party made its way to Yellowstone, which had become a full-scale park with rangers and tourists. By the end of September the weather had turned cold and snow fell almost daily. One morning Jackson and Hayden were riding ahead of the others when they saw a bear almost concealed behind thick shrubbery. Jackson dismounted, unslung his rifle, and advanced toward the animal's hiding place.

"Jack, watch out!" Hayden called in alarm.

As the huge silver-tip grizzly came charging out of the bushes with red eyes glaring, Jackson dropped on one knee and fired his gun. The grizzly collapsed.

"Beautiful shot!" called Hayden, coming toward him.

"Weighs over a thousand pounds if'n he weighs an ounce," said one of the packers when the rest of the party arrived.

That fall, Jackson often relived the encounter as he watched his small son, Clarence, playing with the bear claws brought back as a souvenir. But more often his thoughts turned to the future of his family—expanded by Louise's birth in November. With two small children Emilie deserved more help than she got from a husband away from home for half of each year.

Money for its own sake had never been important to him, but now Jackson would need to provide a larger house and educational opportunities for the children. His top salary had been a hundred and seventy-five dollars a month. It wasn't likely to go much higher. Should he resign from the Survey staff and set up a studio of his own? He wasn't sure that he could be content under the skylight of a studio. In the end he had no choice.

Early in 1879 Congress ordered a consolidation and curtailment of Survey activities. It provided no funds for a photographer.

Hayden looked almost as stunned as Jackson felt. "I don't understand it, Jack. Legislators, artists, historians, scientists, and newspapermen have all eulogized you as a recorder of the West."

Why hadn't he gone ahead with his plans for locating a studio when he'd first thought about it? Jackson reproached himself as he walked home.

"I'm out of a job," he told Emilie in a staccato voice.

"You resigned?"

"No, Congress just didn't provide any funds for W. H. Jackson."

"It—it doesn't seem possible," she said in a choked voice. Then, with a comforting gesture, she added, "Probably it is all for the best. I feel sure you'll just go on to something bigger and better." Emilie's belief in him made unemployment seem more of a challenge than a hardship. As he thought about the Congressional action he realized it had not been personal. The need for surveys was declining.

Two of the biggest considerations in setting up a studio were location and equipment. The latter problem was solved in part when the government let Jackson purchase a thousand dollars' worth of cameras and supplies he'd used on Survey trips for two hundred dollars.

For the place to use this equipment he finally settled on Denver because he liked the climate, the people, and the closeness to the mountains. Railroad magnate Jay Gould promised to recommend him to officials of railroads servicing Colorado.

Emilie and Jackson agreed that it would be best if he went ahead to Denver, got the studio under way, and found a place for the family to live. He took Frank Smart with him. Smart had assisted him on a Survey trip and had become a competent photographer.

In the young, lusty city Jackson set out to look for an appropriate studio. The owner of a building under construction at 413 Larimer Street agreed to put in partitions according to specifications, if Jackson could wait until late August to move in. Delay in getting started in business would mean postponement in bringing the family out, but the location was good and rental reasonable.

"We could, I suppose, work in a boom town during the summer," Jackson told Smart. "Miners and the newly rich are always eager for portraits."

After hearing about the fabulous fortunes being made at Leadville, high in the Rockies, Jackson and Smart set up headquarters there. Dozens of treasure seekers posed in front of Jackson's camera—men with a faraway look in their eyes, who talked about the gold they expected to find over the next hill.

In bad weather Jackson and Smart stayed at a hotel, but most of the time they camped out.

That fall, back in Denver, Jackson watched with pride as the sign went up advertising his studio. As soon as he had proved that he could make a decent living he sent for Emilie. "It's only fair to warn you," he wrote, "that Denver is rough compared to Washington."

"Are you sure we won't be scalped?" Emilie responded teasingly.

After living for a time in a rambling, roomy boarding house, the Jacksons moved to a home of their own. The studio flourished. Besides taking portraits, Jackson sold stereoscopic cards and illustrations for books and magazines. Soon, in addition to Smart, he needed another camera operator, a printer, a mounter, and a receptionist.

In the fall of 1880 a dramatic episode disturbed the Jacksons' usually tranquil life. Tension developed between Denver workmen and Chinese laborers, who poured into the city when the decline in railroad-building and gold-mining left them jobless; and Emilie and Jackson were distressed when their gentle, hard-working laundryman, Lung Fu, told of threats against him. On Sunday, Jackson was reading his newspaper when he heard gunfire some distance away followed by hoots, howls, and the sound of running feet. He hurried to the doorway and saw Clarence, who had been swinging on the garden gate, come scampering toward the porch, and looking very frightened.

Seconds later Lung Fu, with terror etched on his face, hurtled through the gate, behind him a crowd of angry men brandishing sticks and guns. Jackson hastily pushed Clarence and Lung Fu inside the house and closed the door on them. Then, standing on the porch, he faced the crowd alone.

"The Chink's a killer," said a brassy voice. "We're going to string him up."

Jackson had to protect Lung Fu, but he couldn't expose Emilie and his two children to violence. Hoping that the crowd might listen to reason, Jackson held up his hand and said firmly, "If Lung Fu is a criminal, he should be brought before a judge. If he is innocent, I'm sure none of you would want to be guilty of injustice."

Somebody shouted a menacing reply, but a few men at the edge of the crowd turned and went out of the yard. Thus deserted, the accusers became uneasy, and they too went away. Lung Fu was terrified at the thought of continuing to live in Denver after that, and the Jacksons arranged for his passage home to China.

16: *At Home and on the Rails*

JACKSON found life in Denver interesting and stimulating. Walking to his studio each day he took different routes so he could observe the schools, hospitals, and business buildings rising with great rapidity. His Survey pictures had established his reputation. After viewing the photograph of the Mount of the Holy Cross, the poet Henry Wadsworth Longfellow had written a poem that opened:

> There is a mountain in the distant West
> That, sun-defying, in its deep ravines
> Displays a cross of snow upon its side.

Mining magnates, heads of railroads, and community leaders came to Jackson's studio. These men would have welcomed him in their parlors, but he and Emilie had more interest in their home than in social life. On June 7, 1882, the family increased with the birth of a girl named Hallie. As the children grew older, Jackson observed their progress in school, took them to circuses and on long walks. The upside-down hilarity of a nuthatch, the antics of a puppy delighted him as much as the youngsters. At Christmastime he shared in hiding surprise packages, stringing popcorn to trim the tree, opening the trunk of silks Lung Fu sent each year as an expression of gratitude.

In the summer, whenever possible, Jackson arranged combined picnic and photographic projects. Frequently the family took the train to Palmer Lake, where they rented a boat.

After their picnic lunch, while the children were still tossing food to chipmunks, or to jays swooping down on broad blue wings, Jackson would set up his camera. Clarence always stayed close to him, asking questions and handing him supplies, while the girls strayed off, picking flowers to press. Later, Emilie would arrange the pressed flowers in a scrapbook for which Jackson sketched or painted in a background of the places where the plants had been found. He also drew appropriate settings for the poems and descriptive articles on nature that Emilie sold to the *Friends Intelligencer.*

During the 1880s railroads extended secondary lines into remote regions to new settlements and mining towns. Officials wanted photographs to encourage tourist travel. Jackson, interested in railroads almost as much as in cameras, enjoyed supplying illustrations for magazines and promotion folders. Much of his photography was of the narrow-gauge lines. These roads with a space of only three feet between the rails were built to accommodate small, two-engine trains hauling supplies up to mountain mining towns and carrying ore down.

To get pictures along the shining rails that snaked their way along narrow ledges flanked by forests and gorges, Jackson sometimes rode flatcars. But when he photographed for the Denver and Rio Grande he more often than not traveled in a private car provided for his use. Plate-glass mirrors, walnut, and red plush gave it the appearance of a living room.

The whole family would be elated when Jackson would announce, "Pack your bags. This time you're going with me."

"I feel like a pampered aristocrat," Emilie would say as they ate the quail, porterhouse steak, and Rocky Mountain trout served to them while they rolled past breath-taking canyons or across spidery trestles. Jackson would point out places which he had visited on muleback during Survey trips.

For one of the month-long Junkets, Jackson's mother came from the East to go with them. Ignoring wind, smoke, and cinders, she spent many hours on the observation platform apparently enjoying the experience as keenly as her grandchildren.

Scenes of frothy streams, quivering aspens, and sky-reaching peaks, when exhibited outside the state, brought Jackson orders for photographs from other railroad lines, some in foreign countries. At the invitation of the Mexican Central Railway, he went twice to Mexico. On the second trip there he climbed smoking, snow-capped Popocatepetl to take pictures of the volcanic cone. The evergreens and blue lupines that bordered the rough road used by sulphur carriers and timber cutters reminded him of the Colorado Rockies.

In 1887 the family moved into a new home on Clarkson Street in a sparsely settled section of Denver. While Emilie attended to domestic details, Jackson painted fireplace screens and landscapes for the walls. He also built horizontal bars for the children to play on in the back yard.

Proud of their new home, the Jacksons entertained many

friends. Senator H. M. Teller was a frequent visitor, as was ex-Governor William Gilpin, a distant cousin of Emilie's. The children loved to hear the slender, white-haired Gilpin tell about his experiences while exploring with Frémont or fighting in the Mexican War.

The dry plates, improved films, and more compact cameras developed in the late 1880s added to Jackson's pleasure in photography. Clarence took as much interest as he did in new equipment, techniques, and procedures. "Don't be satisfied with shoddy work," Jackson admonished his son when they worked together. "Always give the best you have, whether you're taking the picture of a miner or a millionaire."

Clarence was a highly sensitive boy, and his father and mother became increasingly concerned because he stammered. Thinking it might be easier for him, Jackson enrolled Clarence in a private school operated by Friends at Newton Square, Pennsylvania. Later the boy went to Harned Academy in Plainfield, New Jersey.

Jackson missed his son, but the demands of his business kept his mind occupied. Orders from railroads and hotels for pictures advertising their scenic attractions piled high on Jackson's desk. Earnings spurted ahead when his younger sister Emma moved to Denver to work in the studio as a colorist.

One day as they were finishing a project Emma said, "Do you realize that the Jacksons haven't been together as a family since you and Ed came home that time after the battle of Gettysburg?"

This remark led Jackson to arrange a reunion in Denver in

June 1892 to celebrate the Golden Wedding anniversary of his alert and active parents. Emilie was as pleased as Bill at the success of the family get-together. Fred was still a photographer, Ed a farmer, Allen a musician. Mary Elizabeth, known fondly as Libby, had married a minister.

That fall, Major Joseph Gladding Pangborn, publicity representative of the Baltimore and Ohio Railway, asked Jackson to go East to take some pictures along the railroad's right-of-way. "We'll provide a private railroad car and ten dollars a photograph," he wrote. "The pictures will be displayed in a special exhibit at the Columbia Exposition in Chicago next year."

When Jackson arrived in the East, the pompous, three-hundred-pound Pangborn announced his intention of accompanying him. An adroit and polished ex-journalist, Pangborn was a prime promoter. One day while the two men were aboard the private car somewhere in central New Jersey, Pangborn lighted a big black cigar and then said, "Jack, I'm going around the world and I've decided you should be my camera-man."

He went on outlining a plan to set up a transportation commission to collect models and photographs of transportation both past and present. These would be combined with the Chicago Exposition transportation exhibit.

"Where is the money coming from?" asked Jackson after Pangborn had given the details of what promised to be an elaborate journey.

"Well, you can't, of course, work up anything this big overnight," Pangborn admitted reluctantly. "But men like Pullman and Marshall Field should be interested."

"If you can finance a commission," said Jackson, "I'll be your photographer."

The round-the-world jaunt sounded utterly fantastic. Yet Jackson knew that Pangborn did have unusual talent for carrying out grandiose schemes. Would anything come of the daring dream?

17: *Royal Guest in India: Prisoner in Singapore*

Jackson had no further word from Pangborn. He assumed that the plans for a round-the-world tour had collapsed and so turned his attention to more pressing affairs. For the Baltimore and Ohio exhibit at the Columbia Exposition in Chicago he sent over a hundred of his own landscapes.

On August 23, 1893, Jackson, accompanied by friends who had suggested the stunt, celebrated the twentieth anniversary of his first photograph of the Mount of the Holy Cross by again scaling Notch mountain. Clarence, who had finished his schooling in the East and had been working at the studio, assisted with the photography. For one of the pictures Jackson posed his son on the exact spot from which he had sighted the cross.

"No one except a handful of trappers, Indians, and miners thought the snowy cross existed," he told Clarence. Now people all over the country had seen pictures of it on stereo slides or postcards, many of which were copies of his photographs.

A short time after the trip up Notch mountain, Jackson received an invitation from the Columbian Exposition Commission to make a photographic record of the Fair to incorporate in their final report. He would make the pictures while the exhibits remained intact, but after the gates had been closed to visitors.

"I dislike taking time away from the studio," Jackson told Emilie, "but I need the money." Some months before, he had incorporated with Walter F. Crosby, a wealthy amateur photographer, and leased the two top floors of the Industrial Building. The partners had chosen a poor time to expand. Monetary policies of the government, widespread drought, decline in exports had brought unemployment and national depression.

Jackson took Clarence with him to Chicago. The white façades of the Exposition buildings still looked impressive, but the flags were furled, the fountains lifeless, the hurdy-gurdies silent. One day while Jackson was photographing an exhibit Major Pangborn came striding toward him, beaming like a man who had inherited a million dollars. He explained that before the end of the Exposition the Baltimore and Ohio Railroad had donated its exhibit, including fifty-six model locomotives and nearly two thousand pictures, to Mr. Marshall Field for permanent display in the Fine Arts Building. In return, Mr. Field had contributed twenty-five thousand dollars for a study of transportation. The Major, with the impressive title of head of the World Transportation Commission of the Field Columbian Museum, had already set up an office in the Fine Arts Building.

"It will probably take several months to get the tour completely financed and organized," he told Jackson, "but contributions are pouring in, and I'm counting on you as our photographer."

"Sounds great," said Jackson, "but I'll have to talk it over with my wife."

"Tell her you're indispensable," said Pangborn as he turned and walked away.

That night Jackson saw in a local newspaper an account of an interview with Pangborn, who had described the process of the round-the-world tour as photographing and collecting items related to the history of transportation—everything from carts to railroads, Chinese junks to steamships. "The Major seems sure I'm going," Jackson said to Clarence. "Listen to this: 'W. H. Jackson of Denver, the great photographer, will be official photographer for the commission.' "

"It looks," said Emilie, after Jackson had returned to Denver, "as if I'd exchanged being a Survey widow for being a Transportation Commission widow." But the good-will aspect of his visiting many nations and people appealed to her, and she seemed prepared to make the best of the situation.

Not knowing when the tour might begin, Jackson entered into a whirlwind of preparations. Clarence and Emma would hold the studio together, but he engaged W. H. Rhodes of Philadelphia to serve as general manager. So that Emilie would have less responsibility Jackson explored the possibility of sending Hallie and Louise to a private school in the East, and finally a school near Philadelphia was decided on. Satisfied that his family would be well cared for, he turned his attention to the Exposition pictures. H. H. Tammen, owner of a curio shop and a personal friend, paid a thousand dollars for a duplicate set of photographs and another five thousand for the right to reproduce them in a collection called *The White City*. The folio won so much favorable publicity that Jackson selected thirty-six of his thirty thousand negatives for a book without words. Reviewers had high praise—"Comparable to Mendelssohn's 'Song without Words' . . . "Great photographs by the world's greatest photographer."

But much that happened during the winter of 1893–1894 built up restlessness and unhappiness within Jackson. Emilie's cousin, ex-Governor Gilpin, died, the depression continued, and Pangborn kept delaying the starting time for the trip.

Early in September 1894, Pangborn wrote that the Commission would leave late that month. "There's just one thing," he added, apparently as an afterthought. "In the revised calculations no allowance seems to have been made for your salary. But, of course, all expenses will be paid, and think of the publicity!"

Jackson didn't see how he could possibly take the trip on this basis. The way things were going, the studio wouldn't provide for the family in his absence and Louise and Hallie were already enrolled in the Pennsylvania school. Then it occurred to him that he might get a contract with some magazine for publication of pictures taken during the tour.

Harper's Weekly agreed to use photographs and to pay a hundred dollars a page, if Jackson would provide pictures of landscapes and the every-day life of native people as well as pictures of boats, trains, sampans, and rickshas.

Good-bys to Emilie and the children were even more difficult than Jackson had expected them to be. Even on Survey trips the miles between him and Emilie had seemed endless. Now he would be separated from her by strange seas, scorching deserts, and tall mountain ranges.

The World Transportation Commission, which included Pangborn, Jackson, artist Edward Winchell, mechanical expert Clement Street, and Pangborn's secretary Harry Stevenson, sailed for London late in September. With them they carried official letters of introduction provided by the Secretary of State, Walter Gresham. Newspapers published copies of their intinerary in conjunction with laudatory comments on the aims and personnel of the Commission.

After three weeks of final preparations in London, the Commission traveled to countries bordering the Mediterranean Sea, then through the Suez Canal to Ceylon and India. At Tuticorin, in southern India, the railway officials put a handsome private railway car, *The Rajah,* at their disposal. When they arrived in Bombay on January 19, Jackson thought it one of the most enchanting cities he had ever seen. Negatives piled up faster than he could develop them. The most elaborate entertainment provided for the Commission was a dinner at the Government House as guest of Lord Harris. At the table, Jackson sat next to General Lord Roberts, hero of half a hundred battles.

"I'm beginning to feel like a character in an English novel," Jackson wrote Emilie, "dressing for dinner every night and conversing with Lord this and Lady that. I would prefer the company of *my* Lady Jackson."

From Bombay the Commission went to Karachi on a small

steamer. Then, on land once more, they traveled a route roughly parallel to the Indus River.

On February 8 as the train on which the Commission was riding neared Jammu, winter capital of the Maharaja of Kashmir, Pangborn rose to address the group. "Gentlemen," he said, "this is an important stop. Please remember that you are ambassadors of a great nation."

At the palace the bearded Maharaja, wearing an enormous red turban, a coat heavy with gold braid, and white cotton jodhpurs, welcomed them. Seated on a divan, he questioned the Commission as to their purposes and their intinerary. Then he began talking about watches—mainsprings, jeweled bearings, and makes. "Would you care to look at mine?" he asked.

Jackson expected to see a watch carved with elephants or studded with emeralds, but the one the Maharaja showed them was a nickel-plated Ingersoll!

The Commission left the palace bearing formal invitations to return on February 12. The festivities on Lincoln's birthday began with an elaborate breakfast in a pavilion on the palace grounds. Afterwards, during the review of troops, Jackson took pictures of bearded lancers on black horses, of charging elephants and turbaned artillerymen.

That evening hundreds of tiny lamps—open oil cups with pendant wicks—brilliantly illuminated the palace grounds where the Maharaja sat on a dais. During the fireworks he joined the Commission on a balcony of the palace.

Next day the Commission journeyed to Delhi and Agra, where Jackson photographed the white marble eight-sided Taj Mahal surrounded by lovely gardens and quiet pools reflecting the beauty of the majestic dome and slender minarets.

The Commission reached Calcutta too late for Jackson to attend an international exhibit of photography, but he was told that his panorama of Ouray, Colorado, had won a bronze medal. He hoped to make another prize-winning picture of the Himalayas, but negatives of Mt. Everest, taken from Tiger Hill on a hazy day, produced only a faint image.

Jackson was disappointed by the loss of pictures, but even more by the attitude of Pangborn. At first the Major had done considerable research, dictating page after page of notes to his secretary. But, intrigued by publicity and entertainment, he lost interest in transportation.

"The Commission's trip has deteriorated into a social junket," wrote a reporter in an Indian newspaper. He went on to say that constructive, serious work was being done by the photographer W. H. Jackson.

By Jackson's birthday on April 4, the Commission had reached Singapore. At the harbor Jackson stood for some time watching Chinese junks, Malay *proas,* and English ships. Then he set up his camera and began photographing them. He looked up, startled, when two soldiers came up to him. One of them, a stern-faced individual, said, "You're under arrest."

"But why?" asked Jackson, completely taken by surprise. "I—"

"Your camera was aimed directly at Fort Palmer," the second soldier told him sharply.

"I didn't even know it was there." Jackson began putting away his equipment. "I'm a member of the World Transportation Commission and—"

"It is forbidden to take pictures in a fortified area." The stern-faced soldier glared at him accusingly. Then he repeated, "You're under arrest."

Jackson shrugged helplessly. It would be better, he decided, not to argue with the soldier. As soon as he had been turned over to a higher official, he would ask him to get in touch with Pangborn and the American Consul.

The soldiers took Jackson to Fort Palmer, confiscated his camera, and locked him in a room by himself. Every time he heard footsteps in the corridor, he expected someone would free him and lead him to an official for questioning.

As hours passed, annoyance turned to frustration and anxiety. Had they forgotten him? At last he became genuinely alarmed. What if Fort Palmer had appeared on the negative and the officials had concluded that he was a spy?

A soldier finally entered the room where Jackson had been imprisoned and led him to a police sergeant.

"You'll have to stand trial," the sergeant told him, "but I'll summon the American Consul in your behalf."

The magistrate who heard the case quickly dismissed the charges and returned Jackson's camera.

18: *By Sledge Across Siberia*

DURING the next five months the Commission visited Australia, New Zealand, the East Indies, China, and Japan. "Geography would come alive for you," Jackson wrote Louise and Hallie, "if you could actually see the boomerangs and kangaroos of Australia, the rice and rickshas of the Orient." In a letter to Clarence he confided his successes and failures in photography, including the worthlessness of about one-fourth of the pictures taken in Australia—the result of defective film.

The Commission shrank to four when Clement Street returned to the United States to attend to personal business. The plan, when the remaining members of the Commission sailed from China on the *Ghazee,* was to visit Korea, about which the world knew very little. Jackson looked forward to becoming the pioneer photographer of the "Hermit Kingdom." But after hearing reports of unrest, violence, and intrigue in Korea, Pangborn decreed that the Commission would sail around the peninsula instead of landing on it.

"But you wanted Korean items for your exhibit," Jackson

objected. "And I need photographs to send to *Harper's Weekly*."

"Too risky," Pangborn told him.

"Why don't I go alone, cross the peninsula on horseback, and catch up with you at the port of Wonsan?" Jackson suggested.

Despite opposition he decided to go ashore, but during the first hours in Korea he had doubts as to whether he had acted wisely. Natives seemed hostile. Unable to speak their language, he had difficulty making his wants known. Finally, he did succeed in buying two sturdy ponies. He packed luggage and equipment on one and then set off astride the other one for Seoul.

The Secretary of the United States Legation, Dr. Horace Newton Allen, warned that the Koreans distrusted any foreigners and that bandits were a constant threat. "To cross the country would be dangerous, if not downright impossible," he warned.

"I still want to try," Jackson said quietly.

Before he went, Allen arranged for an audience with the King. His Majesty, flanked by two chamberlains girded with broad purple sashes, received them in his office. Jackson and Allen advanced slowly and bowed three times.

Through Allen, who spoke Korean, Jackson asked many questions about transportation in the country. The King answered willingly and in turn poured out questions about the Commission, photography, and the United States.

By the time Jackson and Allen left the palace, darkness had

fallen. Eight servants bearing muslin-covered lanterns escorted them. When they reached the Embassy, two men stepped forward with bundles containing presents from the King—two tiger skins, three jade boxes, a number of silken scrolls.

Early Wednesday morning, Jackson left Seoul with Pak-na-won, an English-speaking guide selected by Dr. Allen. Rough roads and the beauty of the scenery that kept tempting Jackson to reach for his camera made travel slow. At night Pak usually made arrangements for them to stay in some hovel where they needed the flea powder Dr. Allen had wisely sent with them. Dr. Allen had also provided a glowing letter of introduction, and in many straw-thatched villages the residents turned out to greet the "American photographer."

In Chi-ul-won the benign-looking magistrate Yi-Ung-Yul invited Jackson to his palace for the night. Seated cross-legged on the floor, the two men dined on a peculiar combination of honey, meal, and water, followed by a sort of aspic with dried fish, eggs, chicken, rice, and relishes.

Next morning, Yi-Ung-Yul accompanied Jackson for some distance. Four men blowing long copper trumpets and four others carrying pikes with blue and white flags preceded them. As the heralds sang out, "Ke-hue-chi-roo," respectful townspeople lined the streets.

By the time Jackson reached Wonsan on Sunday, Korean newspapers were referring to him as the "great American Ambassador." Aboard the *Ghazee* once more he gave Pangborn and his colleagues an enthusiastic account of the cordiality with which he had been received. "And I have a splendid set of pictures for *Harper's*," he concluded.

The Commission disembarked at Vladivostok, on October 8. While they were there, news came that Korean rebels, under Japanese influence, had murdered the Queen and imprisoned the King, Jackson thought of Dr. Allen, Yi-Ung-Yul, and Pak, and hoped their lives would not be endangered.

At Khabarovsk, where the Commission had planned to begin their trans-Siberian sledge journey, an officer told them, "You will not be able to continue by troika as planned. The Amur River, which serves as a highway in winter, is not yet frozen."

Since the Trans-Siberian Railway did not yet span the country, the Commission had no choice but to wait. Trying to make good use of his time, Jackson photographed, studied French, and practiced speaking Russian with the natives. He also did some writing, since the editors at *Harper's Weekly* had requested more explanatory material to accompany his pictures.

In a letter to Emilie, Jackson described a great-roofed Russian Orthodox church with beet-shaped spires. "The service was conducted by a tall-hatted priest bedecked in purple velvet and white silk," he wrote.

Jackson had always envisioned Siberia as a cruel, cold land peopled by exiles and their guards. He saw this aspect of the country when he went to photograph the winter quarters of convicts. But he was also invited to many homes where people conversed on art, literature, and politics around tables set with fine china. At one of these gatherings he met hearty, good-natured M. Schimkevitch, who became his friend. Although the Russian made his living as an official of the government, his real interest lay in photography.

"The Mongolian fishing village of Sup-chee-kee would offer unusual pictorial material," he told Jackson. "It would be only a five-hour sledge trip from here. Would you like to go?"

Jackson, bored by the delay imposed on him, accepted eagerly.

At Sup-chee-kee the two photographers soon won the confidence of the villagers. The head man invited them to his own two-room thatch-roofed house, where the eight members of the family shared a savory sturgeon soup. Afterward the family and some of their friends, both young and old, danced to the accompaniment of drums, bells, and tin cans banged together.

Next day Jackson photographed fishermen, dogs, dancers, and the *shaman,* or medicine man, who wore a string of bells and thin brass plates on top of his clothing. Jackson and Schimkevitch had roused so much friendly interest that when they prepared to leave the whole village turned out to give them a rousing send-off.

Word finally came that the Amur River had frozen. The townspeople of Khabarovsk planned a series of parties for the Commission, climaxed by an elaborate banquet. On the morning of December 5, Jackson donned his fur cap, heavy felt boots, and elkskin greatcoat which came clear to his feet and down over his hands. Besides the Commission, the party included two drivers and a minor post official, Karaulov, who spoke English and would serve as courier.

"Ride with me, Jack," Pangborn invited as he settled himself in a *pavoska,* a sturdy narrow sledge with closed top.

Jackson squeezed into the sledge, which was crammed with photographic supplies, luggage, and emergency food supplies —mostly vegetable soup frozen into blocks. Winchell, Stevenson, and Karaulov crowded into the second *pavoska,* which was drawn by three horses abreast.

The sledges took off in a blinding swirl of snowflakes. Their goal, Krasnoyarsk, lay three thousand miles away. Jackson's thoughts sped back to the night he and Rock and Crowl were about to begin the trek to Virginia City. He could almost hear old Dan saying, "It's distance that makes men fall apart the most." The three thousand miles across a wilderness of snow and ice, where temperatures averaged about twenty degrees below zero, suddenly seemed almost terrifying.

The sledge windows soon became so frost-coated that Jackson could not see the ragged dots of falling snow. The drivers of the *pavoskas* followed the route of the Imperial Mail. At post stations, about fifteen miles apart, the men could get out and unkink their muscles. While the horses were being changed, the Commission went inside and took off their burdensome coats. The proprietor, usually a farmer who had little to do during the winter, would rush up to them with tall glasses of hot tea. Food followed—meat or fish, eggs, and soup. If the Commission reached a city at nightfall, they stayed at a hotel. Otherwise they napped in their sledges.

At the end of the fifth day, Jackson, tired of being in the airless *pavoska* with Pangborn, bought a sled with an open front. At times the icy air slashed like a scimitar, but he reveled in the tingle at the bottom of his lungs, and the silvery spray of snow kicked up by the hoofs of the horses. Because of the cold he could do very little photography except when the Commission stopped in cities.

The long trek across the snow ended at Krasnoyarsk. On Monday, January 22, the Commission left by rail for Moscow, as guests of Prince Khikov, Imperial Minister of Communications. At night, huge bonfires illuminated the frozen rivers. Not until Sunday did the Commission reach Moscow.

Pangborn had made it known several weeks earlier that the sponsors had lost interest in sending the Commission through Europe and South America as originally planned. But he had not indicated exactly where or when the tour would end. Now he stated that after a brief inspection of transportation in St. Petersburg the Commission would disband.

In St. Petersburg Jackson selected an unusual brooch for Emilie and handwrought pins for the girls. For Clarence's present he planned a scrapbook with photographs of the trip. Pangborn decided to stay on and tour Europe with his wife and daughter, who had come to join him. Jackson, Winchell, and Stevenson went to Bremerhaven, Germany, where they took a liner that put them into New York on March 3, 1896. They had traveled over a hundred thousand miles.

Jackson wished that by some trick of magic he could be transported immediately to Denver. Home, he thought, as the train carried him westward, was more inviting than any place he had seen in the seventeen months he had been away.

19: *Losses and Loneliness*

J ACKSON was overjoyed at the fervor of his family's welcome. Denver newspapers gave a flattering amount of space to his homecoming. But the studio had suffered. Even after Jackson took over again, business continued to be slow. Denverites had not yet recovered from the after-effects of the Panic of 1893, and they had very little money to spend on photographs.

Increase in circulation of illustrated magazines cut down the sale of negatives. Many of the pictures in these periodicals had been copied from Jackson's photographs, unprotected by copyright. Halftone engraving processes also gave competition. Jackson could make only one print at a time; photo engravings could be turned out by the thousand.

When a professional program manager suggested that Jackson give illustrated talks on the countries he had visited, he welcomed the opportunity to add to his income. Emilie helped him to choose a hundred and twenty-five pictures around which he built a lecture titled *100 Minutes in Strange Lands.* Audiences in various Colorado towns responded with enthusiasm, but advertisements, expense of travel, rental of halls, and payment of his manager ate up the bulk of Jackson's income from the sale of lecture tickets.

"At least the tour earned more widespread recognition for you and your photography," Emilie said to comfort him.

The publicity helped in negotiations with the newly formed Photochrom Company of Detroit, headed by William A. Livingstone. The managers, under supervision of the Detroit Publishing Company, had bought rights to a Swiss-developed photo-lithographic process that made it possible to turn out multiple copies from one hand-colored negative. To get under way in producing everything from post cards to pictures large enough to frame and hang on the wall, Photochrom needed a number of negatives. Jackson had the largest collection ever assembled by one man.

Photochrom offered him five thousand dollars cash, twenty-five thousand dollars, worth of stock in the company, and a position as a salaried director of the firm. Jackson did not like the idea of giving up his Denver studio and of cutting down on his photographic trips. Both he and Emilie resisted selling their home and breaking ties with friends. But the photo-lithographic process intrigued Jackson. How often he had longed for color film that would give his landscapes the blues, yellows, greens, and reds he saw in nature. Emma and Clarence did excellent hand tinting, but it was slow, tedious, and expensive. The new process would not only reproduce his pictures in color but give them wider circulation.

In the end, he and Emilie decided to accept the offer, and in 1898 went to live in Detroit. Emma, who had accepted a position as colorist, joined him at the plant.

That summer Jackson went to Omaha to make a pictorial record of the Trans-Mississippi Exposition. From there he journeyed to the Black Hills to do promotional photography for the Chicago and Northwestern Railroad. He arrived in Deadwood only a week after Clarence, who had been there doing a similar job for another railroad. One night he picked up a local newspaper and was amused when he read:

"A Mr. W. H. Jackson of Detroit has been making pictures in the vicinity for the C. and N. W. Railroad. Incidentally, Mr. Jackson is the father of the celebrated photographer Clarence S. Jackson of Denver, Colorado, who recently was in our midst."

Chuckling to himself, Jackson cut out the item and mailed it to Clarence with a note reading, "Well, son, I see you have arrived. If there is a back seat in your wagon, please reserve it for me."

During the next few years, Jackson spent most of his time at the plant. But to accumulate new pictures for Photochrom he traveled from Maine to California and from Quebec to Cuba. He photographed sugar and cotton plantations in the South, a spectacular roundup in Texas, boats on the St. Lawrence, missions and giant redwoods in California. When Photochrom decided in 1902 to send out a traveling display of their work to be housed in a private car of the Santa Fe Railway, Jackson toured the Southwest aboard the "California Special." At every stop he gave informal talks and answered the questions of those who came to view the exhibits.

In the spring of the following year, Superintendent E. H. Husher resigned from the Photochrom Company. Almost overnight Jackson, then sixty, was elevated to the post of manager of a plant that employed about forty artisans and a dozen traveling salesmen. Through these men, and retail salesrooms in New York, Los Angeles, London, and Zurich, Photochrom sold around a million prints a year.

Jackson enjoyed having more time with his family. He shared Hallie's interest in art and Louise's in music and went on picnics at Belle Isle Park. But more and more often Jackson and Emilie did things alone, while the girls went off with young men likely to become future husbands. Hallie, although the younger, was first to marry.

For a time after the girls had left, the house seemed unbearably empty. The sense of family ties coming unknotted was even more acute after the death of Jackson's father. To get his mind off his own troubles, Jackson joined the ranks of those working to salvage and preserve the cliff dwellings of Mesa Verde. Unless the lost cities could be supervised, souvenir hunters would wreck them. When Congress finally made Mesa Verde a national park in 1906, Jackson hoped that visitors would experience at least a little of the solemnity he had felt that night when he had first heard the wind sighing through the silent city on the ledge.

With more leisure than he had ever had in his life, Jackson learned to play golf. The high-wheeled contraptions with a one-cylinder motor under the seat that chugged, chuffed, and backfired on Detroit's Grand Boulevard provided another hobby.

"She'll travel up to twenty-miles an hour," he told Emilie proudly after he had driven home a Model T Ford. "And listen to this." Boyishly he grasped the hand horn, which gave a loud bleat. On Sundays, wearing a duster and goggles, Jackson, with Emilie at his side, rode off to photograph new scenes. If when he cranked the car it started with reluctance—or not at all, as was often the case—Jackson would remind himself that he'd still rather rely on an automobile than a bull or a burro.

In 1912 his mother died at the age of ninety-two. Jackson's grief was softened by thoughts of her long, useful life. Memories of her painting lessons that had helped him to choose his profession impelled him to a new outburst of photographic activity apart from his heavy managerial responsibilities at Photochrom.

Jackson's energy, as well as his photography, attracted the respect and friendly interest of Henry Ford, creator of the Model T.

"What makes you tick anyway?" Ford asked one day.

"Always having something to do," Jackson replied.

The doing increased with American entry into World War I on April 6, 1917. With fellow Detroiters Jackson joined in Liberty Loan drives, "Food for Victory" gardens, and the anxious scanning of reports from the battlefront. Clarence was too old to go, grandson William Henry was too young, but Jackson sympathized with the anxiety of parents who had draft-age sons.

When rumors of an armistice began to filter through, Jackson, along with other war-weary Americans, rejoiced that peace would soon be a reality. "We'll do something to celebrate," he told Emilie. "Maybe we'll take a trip."

"That would be nice," said Emilie. But as Bill studied her thin, pale face, he thought she was less responsive than usual.

Shortly before the Armistice, Emilie died. Jackson tried to dwell on the loving companionship which had been his for forty-five years. But such remembrances could not make him forget that he was seventy-five and alone. The old restlessness that had set him to wandering from Vermont to California across mountains, prairies, and deserts seized him once more.

Jackson's daughter Louise, who with her children, now fatherless, had moved to Detroit during the war, managed his home. Complying with the requests of his three grandchildren to read to them, to play games, or take them for a ride kept him from complete desolation. But the future no longer beckoned.

During the winter of 1920–1921 an economic recession developed. Although minor, it hit the Photochrom Company hard. Jackson, responsible more for technical than financial aspects of production, could do little. Early in 1924 the company collapsed. Photochrom owed him over six thousand dollars in back salary. He had no savings to draw upon because instead of banking his earnings he had invested in additional shares of stock in the company.

Trained in frugality by early wartime and trail life, Jackson managed to live on the pension he received as a veteran of the Civil War. But his daughter Hallie worried about him and kept urging him to move to her home in Washington, D.C.

In the autumn of 1924, Jackson yielded to her persuasion. For hours on end he photographed, painted, and talked to friends at the Cosmos Club, a philosophical society. With artist W. H. Holmes, Director of the National Gallery and formerly a member of the Hayden Survey team, Jackson reminisced about experiences of camp and saddle.

Jackson had found living with Hallie, her husband Myron Pattison, and their two daughters very pleasant, but he wanted to do intensive research on the old West. This necessitated almost daily trips to the Library of Congress and the National Museum. To be close to these centers of information he rented a room at the Annapolis Hotel.

Personal knowledge supplemented by careful research made Jackson an authority on the old West. Museums consulted him; editors solicited not only photographs but articles. For a book on his photographic experiences, Jackson collaborated with Dr. Howard R. Driggs, Professor of English at New York University.

"You're becoming a celebrity all over again," Hallie said, teasing, when *The Pioneer Photographer* was published in 1929.

20: *Too Busy to Die*

IN 1929, although he was then eight-five, Jackson accepted a post as Research Secretary for the Oregon Trail Memorial Association. This meant a move to New York. The Association, headed by Jackson's friend Dr. Howard Driggs, had been formed to preserve and mark the Oregon Trail, to add to information about it, and to perpetuate its spirit through narrative and paintings.

Jackson handled correspondence, addressed meetings, accumulated data, represented the Association at anniversary celebrations and at dedications of trail monuments. Trail associates fondly dubbed him Mustang Jack.

He traveled extensively during vacations as well as when involved in trail business. One summer he went with the Colorado Mountain Club for an exploration of the Elk Mountains and easily held his own. In August 1935 he flew from St. Joseph, Missouri, to Washington, D.C. Boy Scouts, celebrating the seventy-fifth anniversary of the Pony Express, had ridden in relays over the old route from Sacramento, California, to St. Joseph, Missouri. The message they carried was handed over to a group of celebrities waiting to take it by plane to President

Franklin Delano Roosevelt. Jackson was among those selected to ride in the plane and to present the message and commemorative gold medal to the President.

Jackson's paintings were receiving almost as much recognition as his photographs. After Driggs had begged him to paint the West as he had known it he had turned to his long neglected brushes. His pictorial maps and paintings of incidents of the westward movement were exhibited in national park museums.

"Superb," said critics, "whether considered from the standpoint of quality, subject matter, historical value, or beauty."

Arno B. Cammerer, Director of the National Park Service, asked Jackson to paint four murals for the museum in the new Department of the Interior Building. Because Jackson was then ninety-two, Cammerer had to get special permission because of his age. The work would have to be fitted in between duties connected with the Oregon Trail Association. Before doing any painting on the murals that would memorialize the work of four projects in the early days of the Geological Survey, Jackson studied survey reports, journals, and old photographs.

He enjoyed working on the murals as much as anything he had ever done in his life. For the Wheeler Survey of 1873, he depicted the party camping near a Zuni pueblo; for the Powell Survey he showed men working along the canyon floor of the Colorado River. The Sierra Nevada mountains formed the background for King's Survey of the Fortieth Parallel. With almost every brush stroke of the Hayden party, with Old Faithful in the background, Jackson relived incidents of the summer in Brimstone Basin.

On the day the murals were unveiled, Park Service officials gave a reception for the artist. Reporters praised the paintings as "history documented in pictures . . . The West interpreted with a spirit few have equaled."

Besides painting, writing, photographing, participating in Oregon Trail activities, and Explorers' Club fellowships, Jackson appeared before historical societies, campfire groups in national parks, service clubs, and Republican rallies across the country. He especially liked speaking to students. Bits of philosophy were wedged in between tales of bullwhacking, Korea, Paiutes, and photography. "Think more of giving than of getting," he would tell youthful admirers. "Be moderate in your habits and never carry any hatred in your hearts."

Honors poured in upon Jackson. The Royal Photographic Society of Great Britain elected him to honorary membership. Photographs exhibited in London, Calcutta, and Paris won medals. Edsel Ford bought his collection of almost forty thousand glass negatives and donated them to the Dearborn Museum as the W. H. Jackson Historical Collection.

When several of his old pictures won prizes for "pictorial and technical excellence" at a competitive exhibit at the Explorers' Club, Jackson was amazed. He had photographed these scenes before some of the judges were born, he told his son Clarence, and he had used slow lenses, glass plates, and hand-applied emulsions.

Still intent on improving techniques, Jackson experimented with color photography and was elated by the results. The small, light-weight Leica camera delighted him. Asked to divulge his secrets of successful picture making to photographic groups, he would say, "Use the best possible equipment, be patient, watch the smallest details. Above all, be willing to work hard, and to give the best you have."

On Jackson's ninety-fourth birthday, April 4, 1937, he gave an illustrated account of his sledge trip across Siberia at an Explorers' Club dinner in his honor. He used his Civil War bayonet to cut the huge birthday cake bearing ninety-four candles and a map of the Oregon Trail. The first piece went to his grandson Allan Jackson.

In June of that year he traveled to Boulder to receive from the University of Colorado a Recognition Medal for service to the nation. Historian Dr. Colin B. Goodykoontz in his presentation speech on June 14 paid tribute to Jackson's efforts in behalf of Yellowstone and Mesa Verde parks, to his contributions to anthropology and ethnology, and to his efforts in behalf of the Oregon Trail Association. In conclusion Dr. Goodykoontz referred to him as "a pioneer in the preservation and representation of the beauties of untamed nature in our great West."

Later, Jackson went on to Cheyenne. Attracted by a photographic display in a store window, he overlooked an open doorway and landed on his back ten feet below.

"It seems ironical," he told the physician at the hospital, "that I could have fought a war, bullwhacked, ridden wild horses, and traveled halfway around the world unharmed, and then fall into a cellar and crack vertebrae."

Five weeks later, although still suffering some discomfort, Jackson left the hospital and resumed his writing, painting, travel, and photography.

When the Department of Interior staged an exhibit of his life's work, Jackson participated in the sound reel recording the events. Although reticent about his personal life, he tried to be patient under questioning. When one reporter asked him for the secret of his success, he replied, "I never took a sufficiently long vacation to let my go-power run down."

Asked about hardships he had encountered, Jackson said, "There weren't any to speak of."

The hardest blow had been losing Emilie. Within him there would always be an aching core of loneliness, but this loneliness was eased through association with friends. He made new ones readily, but never neglected the old ones.

In late June of 1939 Jackson swapped yarns with Civil War veterans tenting at Gettysburg. With another Union soldier and two Rebels he flew in a plane strewing roses over the cemetery where Vermonters had fallen in battle. He saw President Roosevelt dedicate the Eternal Light.

The following January the Explorers' Club gave a testimonial dinner for Jackson. After a number of friends had spoken admiringly of "that cameraman Jackson," Ernest Ingersoll, reporter-naturalist on the Mesa Verde Survey trip who had remained a comrade through the years, rose and said, "What we all want to know is why you've lived so long and so youthfully."

"I'm too busy to die," Jackson smiled impishly. "Always have something to do tomorrow," he advised. "New ventures keep you spry."

His newest venture, writing an autobiography requested by G. P. Putnam's Sons, at times staggered him. How could he pack almost a century of busyness and adventure into the three hundred and fifty pages allotted him?

"Lively, informative, and a notable book, particularly for a man in his nineties," said a reviewer when *Time Exposure* was published in 1940.

Release of the book set off a round of interviews in New York and later in Denver, Colorado Springs, and at the University of Wyoming, where Jackson went to receive an honorary Doctor of Law degree. Reporters described him as clear-eyed, courtly, dapper, and bubbling with good humor. "A mind as accurate as his camera," wrote one reporter.

Despite all his activities, Jackson had managed to keep in close touch with his children and grandchildren. Each year for his birthday as many as could come assembled at Hallie's home in Chevy Chase, Maryland, at Louise's in Detroit, or at Clarence's in New York. For his ninety-eighth birthday Jackson, Clarence, and Louise visited Hallie and Myron Pattison. The family had just sat down at the table when the doorbell rang. Myron, who went to answer, found reporters wanting a news story.

With a sigh Jackson excused himself from the table and went into the living room to face the representatives of the press. Asked about the future of photography he replied, "Who knows? What man can imagine, he can achieve."

At the conclusion of the interview one of the reporters said, "I hope I'm around when you reach your hundredth birthday."

"I expect you will be," Jackson quipped. "You look reasonably healthy."

Shortly after the birthday celebration, Clarence urged

Jackson to come to live with him and his wife. "We'd fix up working and living space for you," he promised.

Jackson sat silent for a moment; then he said, "Son, I appreciate your offer more than I can say. Maybe some day when I'm old, I'll come, but thank you anyway."

One day in June 1942, Jackson was alone in his room at the Latham Hotel in New York painting one of his favorite scenes in Wyoming in the vicinity of Laramie Peak and La Bonté Creek. In this as in every picture he painted he was trying to recapture the mystery, grandeur, and space of the West. Jackson stood back to study the wagon train descending toward the stream of water at sunset, when dizziness overtook him and he fell to the floor. The sun of his life was setting and he died on June 30.

New York papers headlined the death of the "grand old man of photography." Said Dean Embree, vice president of the Trails Association, "One could not know him without having been a better man for it."

Jackson's work represented all that is finest in the tradition of his profession. His paintings and photographs of peaks, plains, bullwhackers, surveyors and chiefs hang in schools, universities, libraries, railroad stations, and museums. They also illustrate many books, including *Picture Maker of the Old West,* written by his son Clarence. His diaries, articles and *Time Exposure* are important contributions to American history. The height from which he took the picture of the snowy cross is now named Mt. Jackson. Other peaks, buttes, a canyon, and a great sparkling lake in Wyoming bear his name.

Out in western Nebraska, where Jackson camped as a bull-whacker, a plaque in the Jackson Memorial wing of the Scotts Bluff National Monument reads:

> To Keep in Memory His Gentle Courageous Spirit,
> His Devotion to America and Its Pioneers
> His Service in Portraying Their Epic Story.

It is a fitting tribute to a man who loved his country and immortalized its beauty and spirit on film and canvas. Whatever William Henry Jackson did, he did to the best of his ability with courage, integrity, and dedication.